S

Please return/renew this item by the
last date shown to avoid a charge.
Books may also be renewed by phone
and Internet. May not be renewed if
required by another reader.

www.libraries.barnet.gov.uk

John Williams

MY SON'S NOT RAINMAN

one man,
one autistic boy,
a million adventures

Michael O'Mara Books Limited

First published in Great Britain in 2016 by
Michael O'Mara Books Limited
9 Lion Yard
Tremadoc Road
London sw4 7nq

A CIP catalogue record for this book is available from the British Library.

Papers used by Michael O'Mara Books Limited are natural, recyclable products made from wood grown in sustainable forests. The manufacturing processes conform to the environmental regulations of the country of origin.

ISBN: 978-1-78243-388-0 in paperback print format
ISBN: 978-1-78243-389-7 in ebook format

2 3 4 5 6 7 8 9 10

Cover design by Estuary English
Typeset by Tetragon, London
Printed and bound by CPI Group (UK) Ltd, Croydon, cro 4yy

www.mombooks.com

This book is dedicated to the memory of Connor Sparrowhawk.
May your legacy be lasting change for all young people.
Shine bright, Connor.

#JusticeforLB
www.justiceforlb.org.uk

CONTENTS

'I would like to travel the world with you twice.
Once, to see the world.
Twice, to see the way you see the world.'

– UNKNOWN

INTRODUCTION

Well, The Boy is a wonder. He's my wonder. Despite the challenges or maybe even because of them, he's the very best thing in the world. You could line up every precious diamond in *Minecraft* and it wouldn't come close to how precious he is. And, of course, I'm biased. But I want people to give him a chance. To look past some of the seemingly strange, challenging behaviours and the outbursts. To chip away at some of the rock and discover this brilliant, dazzling boy inside just waiting to shine. That's why I wanted to tell our story. We only really celebrate disability in this world when there is a skill involved. The Paralympics, amazing though they are, celebrate the ability and aptitude of the athletes. Well, sometimes just 'being' is enough. And we don't celebrate just 'being' enough. Yet often, it's in the smallness, in the everydayness of life that real beauty occurs. And that's what I want all this to be about: a celebration of the everyday, of 'being'.

MY SON'S NOT RAINMAN BLOG

I t was autumn 2011 and I'd been booked as a stand-up comedian for an office party in a London comedy club. From a comedian's point of view, gigs like this are notoriously difficult, full of people who don't really want to be there, apart from the one person in the office who had the brainwave in the first place. The rest of the audience are largely drawn by the prospect of a free bar more than any great desire to be entertained. Still, I was a relative newcomer, at the ripe old age of thirty-nine, and I knew very little about which gigs to avoid or what was a good or bad audience. Someone was willing to pay me to get onstage and tell jokes. Cracking. Let's put what happened next down to naivety.

The thing is, I'd always wanted to talk about my family life when I was onstage. Other comics did it; for many it's the staple of their sets, talking about their wives, their children, the foibles of everyday life. I knew my home life was different in some ways, not least because The Boy's mum and I had separated some years earlier, but I could still share it with people couldn't I? Couldn't I?

The comic before me went down a storm. Stories of screaming toddlers in supermarkets and his wife's inability to understand him; they lapped it up. Then it was my turn. I got onstage, opening with some of my old material that I knew worked, just to get them onside and reassure them that I was funny. I got a round of applause for the first joke, the seal of approval every comic hopes for. They were going to be OK. Now seemed the time to hit them with the new stuff.

'I'm a single dad,' I said, building in confidence, 'which basically means you all think I'm a much nicer person than you did twenty seconds ago.' They laughed at the time, although now it's written down it doesn't seem the funniest of gags, I grant you. We'll put it down to one of those 'you had to be there' moments.

'Why is that?' I continued, the glare of the stage lights beating down on me. 'Why when I mention I'm a single father am I meant to be some kind of hero? Single mothers? You're all benefit-sappers apparently, but single fathers, ooh, we're all heroes. Next year it's me and a war veteran fighting it out at the Pride of Britain Awards.'

They were a good audience. Things were going OK. I relaxed a bit more. I started talking about my son, about the things children do, how they drive you mad sometimes. That familiar sound, the laughter of recognition, filled the room and, shallow as it might sound, a little bit of it filled my heart too. It felt good. I was on a roll. I decided to talk about my home life some more. 'My son,' I said as one joke finished and the laughter was just ebbing away, 'he's autistic.'

Silence.

Time. Stood. Still. Whatever had gone before was suddenly over. Two hundred people just stared at me. The party pooper had put an end to their night. Each blank face looked out at me from the shadows with the same thing written all over it: 'We're having a night out. Why are you telling us this?' I was booked to do twenty minutes that night; I managed seven. I didn't even have a chance to get to the bit about cerebral palsy. I left the stage dejected, broken. They hadn't just rejected me as a comedian, they'd rejected my son too. As I snuck out of the back door I could hear the next comic onstage, talking away about parents' evenings and once again laughter filled the room. I caught the train home, emotions changing with each passing station, from incandescent rage to utter sadness.

I'd like to tell you that by the next day I'd moved on, but it took a fortnight of dwelling on every moment of that night before I eventually picked myself up. And then I cancelled every gig I had booked. (That sounds fairly dramatic – there were only six in the diary. I wasn't quite ready for prime-time Saturday-night television just yet.) If I couldn't find a way to talk about the thing that mattered to me most, then I didn't want to talk about anything at all.

There had to be a way, though. There had to be a way to share our story. Despite my son's diagnosis, and maybe even sometimes because of it, my world is filled with joy and laughter. That was all I ever wanted to get across. He'd faced discrimination at every point of his life to date. If I could only get people to understand him more, maybe, just maybe, that might change.

So, in October 2012, nearly a year after that fateful corporate gig and with my son's age reaching double figures, I started to write a blog, all about him. I referred to him as 'The Boy', primarily to save his blushes, but also because that's what he wanted to be called. And over the next couple of months I began to put together a comedy show about the two of us. I thought if people know the subject matter beforehand, maybe they'd be more open to it. It turned out that there was no 'maybe' about it. People read the blog and came to the shows. Lots of people. And they laughed. In some small way, they shared the joy. It seemed they understood The Boy and accepted him more than I ever thought they would.

This book is just another part of that process – another opportunity to share the highs and lows of our lives together. I don't want it to be just a story about autism; I want it to be about a young boy who happens to have autism – there is a difference. He will forever be more than just his diagnosis. And there's more here, much more. Fundamentally, I want it to be about every brilliant piece of him. I want it to be about belonging, about fathers and sons, about all our childhoods, about turning on a light when the monsters come out at night, about how if you keep looking for what's wrong you might just miss the very thing that's right. I want it to be about laughter, lots of laughter, proper hurting-from-the-belly laughter that comes in waves and then ebbs and flows to live on in memories long after the tears have stopped. I want it to be about love. Bucketloads of the stuff. About discovery, about adventure, about knights slaying dragons, about superheroes, about victory for each and every little man in this world.

And long after I've left this world, I want it to be a book for you, son. Although I've shared so much of it with you over the months I've been writing it, my biggest hope is that one day in the future you might sit down in a quiet moment, turn to the first page and read it all from cover to cover. Know you are loved, precious boy.

This is our story.

CHAPTER ONE

Can't Smile Without You

Today would have been my dad's birthday. He would have been seventy-seven years old. It's hard to comprehend that big, strong man from my childhood ever being such an age. And it's even harder to comprehend that it's been twenty-three years since all his vibrant strength and happiness was extinguished from the world.

I often think about what Dad, if he was able to drop in for an hour, would make of the world nowadays. How alien would it seem to him? The Internet. Twenty-four-hour television. That roundabout near where we used to live which they've replaced with traffic lights.

And, most of all, I wonder what he'd make of his grandson. I know he'd love him dearly, but would he understand him? He probably wouldn't know how to spell the word autism, let alone come to terms with it. And then there's the strangest thing of all, that the two people who have played the biggest part in shaping my life are the two people who will never ever meet.

It was a source of regret from the moment he was born that The Boy would never know his granddad. He'd never know what it felt like to be carried on the shoulders of a 5-foot 10-inch giant with a headful of hair gel, surrounded by the potent odour of Old Spice aftershave and Silk Cut cigarettes. And then one day it occurred to me, that although the two of them will never meet in the physical sense, Granddad is still never very far away.

Son, you know how Dad beeps the car horn and then waves at strangers to see if they wave back? That was Granddad's game. You know when Dad told you that his scar from his tuberculosis jab was where he got shot fighting in the war? Granddad too. The whistling, listening to Frank Sinatra, making you say 'Thank you' when you get down from the dinner table, it's all him. The more I think about it, the more I realize, he's everywhere, in everything I do.

MY SON'S NOT RAINMAN BLOG

There's such an urge to start this story with The Boy's birth, as if the world only began with him and everything that came before was just incidental. But the truth is, this story started way, way before he was even thought of. Before I'd even taken my first step, before anyone in the

Williams family had even begun to imagine the horror of one of their offspring upping sticks from the north-west of England to take root down south, in London. *Of all places.*

It starts with you, Dad.

I don't have many early memories of him. If I'm honest, he wasn't around a great deal when we were growing up. My mum's family ran a catering firm and part of his reward for marrying her was he got to work for them, six days and nights a week, catering for freemasons' halls, weddings, funerals and everything in between. The work was nothing if not varied. I used to go along and help out from the age of thirteen for the princely sum of five pounds. One evening would be a banquet at the town hall, the next would be a traditional hot pot dinner for a Working Men's Club with ladies getting their boobies out and dancing on the stage. I thought it was the best job in the world.

There are certain things that will always evoke memories of Dad: the sight of those small brown wage envelopes you can buy in the pound shop, the same ones that used to magically appear on the mantelpiece behind the carriage clock every Thursday without fail; the sound of a Ford Transit van pulling into a driveway in second gear when it should really be in first but the driver's too tired to shift gear; the clicking sound of the ignition button on a Calor Gas heater first thing on a cold winter morning. They all meant one thing: Dad's home.

It sounds like a horrible way to describe someone, but he wasn't the cleverest of men, I remember that much; although I do recall him telling us proudly that he passed the exam to go to grammar school. Mind you, he also told us that he danced with Sammy Davis Jnr and dated Tina Turner, so you can take that with a pinch of salt. He was, however, a born entertainer, a showman through and through, the boy who never grew up. If ever there had been a demand for a prime-time TV show where someone whistled Johnny Mathis songs while extolling the virtues of brushing your shoes ('Don't forget the heel! You can always spot a lazy bastard as they only polish the front'), he'd have made top billing. But if there's one thing I've learnt over the years, it's that dads-who-never-grow-up make for pretty rubbish husbands.

I was one of four boys. With my dad in the mix, in many ways my poor mum had a fifth child on her hands. And how hurtful it must have been sometimes, when she did everything in terms of bringing us up, to see us get so excited when Dad eventually had a night off. Mr Fun Time was in town.

I remember going on a rare day trip when I was about nine years of age. The whole family went to the Alton Towers theme park. It was so long ago that it was pretty much just a swing and a roundabout in those days. I think the slide might have opened the year after. In fact, it was that long ago that rather than paying at a kiosk (for which you had to wait most of the day) you paid as you drove into the car park. There was a lady sitting in a hut and you'd pull up alongside her and then she'd count the number of heads in the car – four children, two adults, you'd pay the money and then go and park.

I still remember Dad taking the Alton Towers' exit off the M6 motorway in our faithful Nissan Bluebird, then pulling into a lay-by around six miles away. We'd talked about this moment, like we'd always talked about doing a runner in the Beefeater restaurant when the bill arrived. We never thought he was going to go through with it. But when he reached down beside his driver's seat and pulled a lever, the noise of the boot unlocking confirmed our worst fears.

You just trust your dad, don't you? Three of us climbed into the car boot like trusting lambs being led to slaughter. We knew no different. Then Dad placed a blanket over the top of us – 'just in case of spot-checks, lads' – closed the boot and drove the remaining six miles to Alton Towers. He pulled up at the hut with the lady inside; she peered inside the car – two adults and one child. Dad dutifully paid, then parked at the far side of the car park.

I remember that moment so clearly, when he opened the boot. I remember my eyes adjusting to the daylight and the sensation of the hallucinations from the four-star petrol fumes wearing off. And I remember his big, grinning face bearing down on us. He had a look on his face like he'd just smuggled his family across the Gaza Strip.

'Victory for the little man, boys,' he beamed, 'victory for the little man.'

I was nineteen years old when that big, brilliant face of his left us forever.

He'd been ill for most of my teenage life; the years of drinking and smoking had taken their toll. First heart disease and then, eventually, cancer. He came home to die, that was his last wish: to 'put all his affairs in order' I think is the correct term. All that really meant was confessing to my mum that he'd drunk the vodka in the drinks cabinet and replaced it with water so she wouldn't know, and to tell the vicar that he 'didn't want any of that morbid shit' at his funeral. And I'd like to tell you that those final days were a profound, life-changing period in which serenity washed over all our lives, just like in the movies. But in truth they were hideous affairs, when the morphine levels never seemed quite right and his indomitable spirit raged and fought against the failing light. Eventually, eventually, in the dead of night, when all was quiet…

Reading this back, it seems a strange way to start a book, to condense a man's life and death into the first chapter. But my dad had to be the beginning of the story. His sense of humour, his playfulness, they run through my life like the words in a stick of rock. He shaped the father I've become. I don't think as children we ever really know our parents as people – living, breathing people. We just see them as invincible. He was the man who taught me that the real superheroes in this world are often living among us. It was only years later, when I looked back, that I realized he was fallible too. He never thought he was good enough or smart enough.

I don't have much of a memory for dates and times; birthdays, anniversaries, they merge into one. I couldn't tell you where I was when John Lennon died or who won the 2002 World Cup. I can, however, tell you the two dates that have irrevocably changed my life. On 16 October 1991, I said goodnight to my dad for the last time. And then 3,825 days later, on 6 April 2002, I said hello to my son for the first time. These are the two people who have shaped my life, who will never, ever meet, linked only by my own fallible memory and a propensity for weight gain that I'm blaming firmly on genetics.

You did all right, Dad. You did all right.

CHAPTER TWO

Dream On

There are over seven billion people in the world and the chances of two of those people ever coming together to make one... It means that one can never, ever be anything less than extraordinary. I still remember the day he was born, all those years ago. Ten fingers. Ten toes. We hit the jackpot. The Easter bunny, Father Christmas and the tooth fairy had all arrived in town that night and the streets were paved not just with gold but were laden with diamonds and emeralds; the night skies were lit with a thousand stars, and not one of them shone as brightly as that beautiful baby boy did. Dad's got dreams for you, son.

MY SON'S NOT RAINMAN BLOG

I'd heard of other authors coming across stumbling blocks when writing books, pages that stumped them for some time. But surely they got further than the second paragraph of the second chapter before it happened? Especially when the first paragraph was something they'd copied from their blog.

As a result, I've 'come away for the weekend' to try to write. I had visions of Agatha Christie sitting at a real fireplace in a small coaching inn, a hot toddy at her side as the ideas tumbled out of her head on to the page below. It transpires, however, that idyllic coaching inns are at something of a premium at the weekend and so, instead, I find myself in a Wetherspoons pub on the east coast of England, with a pack of fifteen broken pens from the local pound shop, cursing myself for having no companion to partake of the 'two main meals for £7' offer.

You see, it never really dawned on me before I started to tell our story that in so many ways it's easier to write about the dead. I think that's why I started with my dad; the living are far more complicated to deal with. With the living there are other people and feelings to take into account, other lives to be lived, not least The Boy's. And his birth, which I really want to write about, suddenly seems so difficult.

The Boy's mum and I have been separated for around ten years now, but she's very much a part of his life. Mum lives around the corner and the three of us will forever be inter-twined, knotted and wrapped together in it all. However, what I write here can only ever be my view and my perspective on the journey we've been on.

It's strange trying to recall a life with a partner before children; everything seems an entire lifetime away. The idea that the two of you once shared an existence *before them* just seems too strange to comprehend. What on Earth did you do all day long? In the evenings, when work had finished, how did you spend your time? What did you talk about?

I made my big proposal at midnight at the start of the new millennium, 1 January 2000, as the fireworks exploded in the night sky and the first chimes of Big Ben rang in our ears.

It didn't really happen then.

It was my intention to do that, honestly, but I never was any good with surprises or secrets, so I proposed six days earlier, on Christmas Day, instead. I'll come clean, I panicked. We'd exchanged presents that morning and she'd bought me a lot more than I'd bought her. I felt bad. So I gave her the ring. We married fourteen months later in Scotland, on a cold, snowy day in March. And however things might have turned out, years down the line, it was a good day surrounded by family and loved ones. Maybe the best of days.

A honeymoon in Thailand followed. My first (and, as it transpires, last) proper holiday since a memorable 'lads holiday' to Corfu in 1989. I liked Thailand a lot. I'm sure it has changed nowadays, but back then it really was the Land of Smiles. And my status was apparently revered. Here at home in the UK, I was just another overweight man who didn't exercise anywhere near enough and ate far too much, but in Thailand a man of my size was a novelty. I found myself in the realm of Gulliver wherever we went. It turns out that the Thai people had elevated anyone with a BMI of thirty-five or over to the status of 'rich landowner'. I'd finally made it.

Once the initial excitement and confidence boost died down, I soon discovered that such a title earns you very few privileges, apart from being charged double what your new wife is when you go into shops. As a result, the rich landowner spent a large part of his honeymoon on the pavement or hiding round corners.

A fortnight later we were home in time to meet the truck from Debenhams department store dropping off the gifts from the wedding list. What a weird and wonderful concept that was (and still is) – the wedding list. Although it's lovely to ensure you get the presents you want, and grateful though I am, it still troubles me that on what was one of the most significant days of my life to date, my best mate in the entire world bought me a bin. Still, at least I now know what Egyptian cotton is. That, combined with now being in possession of a stoneware casserole dish, meant I had reached a level of maturity that I would not surpass in this lifetime. It could only mean one thing, it was time to have a baby.

I suppose looking back we didn't leave ourselves a great deal of time to enjoy being married before making this decision, but bear in mind that this was some years ago. I smoked, I drank a fair bit and, according to the people of Thailand, I looked like I not only owned but had eaten half of Manchester. Let's just say, I thought things might take a while. They didn't.

The pregnancy itself went OK, at least from my perspective. To be fair though, it was never really going to be the greatest stretch for me. The first few months saw the two of us giddy with excitement. We took out a second mortgage to pay for baby magazines and every day another new book from Amazon, offering fresh insights into this seemingly unheard-of phenomenon called 'childbirth', would land on the doormat. We also compiled a never-ending list of Things We Wouldn't Do That Our Own Mothers Suggested As We Preferred To Listen To The Opinion Of Strangers In Books Who By The Way Always Seemed To Be Australian. Ah, there's nothing quite like the blind arrogance of a first-time pregnant couple. Neither of us really had a clue, but we hadn't known anything about weddings twelve months earlier and now here we were, owners of a Le Creuset griddle pan. I researched prams and car seats. We'd be just fine.

I thought, along with everyone else, that we were having a girl. (I hope I'm not giving too much away but, having seen the title of the book, you've probably worked out for yourself how this one ends). Girls were rare in our family – myself and my three brothers were testament to that. Grandchildren so far had all been boys. If nothing else, the law of averages said we'd have a girl and so did lots of people who claimed that you could tell by the shape of the bump that it's a girl. I suppose deep down, I wanted a girl too. In my simplistic view I thought a girl might take after her mum. She'd be confident and outgoing. But a boy… a boy might inherit all the insecurities of his dad.

Talking of insecurities, as a man, I've felt inadequate at numerous points in my life. There have been moments when situations have overwhelmed me, when the sheer complexity of being a tiny, fragile, minuscule thread within the rich tapestry of life felt like it might blow my mind apart. But nothing, nothing can compare to the inadequacy I felt as a male of the species when I found myself on a labour ward. If the phrase 'surplus to requirements' was invented for a particular moment in one's life, it's this one.

Oh, they tell you how important it is that you're there. All those self-help books say what a difference you'll make to your loved one by holding their hand and offering words of reassurance. Well, gentlemen, let me share with you a little secret. Take it from someone who's been there, someone who has gone over the top, seen things he never thought he would and then returned to tell the tale. All those books you've read, they're lying. Every one of them. From the moment you arrive at the hospital carrying her overnight bag for her so that in some pathetic, credulous way you feel you might be sharing the experience, you are in reality of no use whatsoever to anyone. You fit in like a vegan in a slaughterhouse.

After the first four hours of the two of us being alone in that room, I sensed my endless stroking of the back of her hand was about as soothing as the sensory deprivation tactics deployed in Guantanamo Bay. Realizing what I was doing was maybe a bit much, I instead opted for my second and only other tactic. I asked her for the one hundred and twenty-second time if she wanted me to get her anything. 'Yes,' she replied. Yes! She said

'Yes'! Granted, it was accompanied by a look that suggested her thought might be 'a new husband', but still, she wanted me to get her something. 'A sandwich.'

Finally, I had a purpose. 'What sort?' I asked. I was keen to get it right, this moment that had been one hundred and twenty-two questions in the making.

'Anything, John.' Ah, the John at the end of the sentence told me all I needed to know. It was not a time to debate the topic further. I would leave her to relax in her bed while I took myself off. For now, I had a mission. The hunter-gatherer had to go and perform his best. I was needed. I was important.

As I strode out of the ward, instead of turning right towards the hospital canteen, I headed towards the main entrance of the hospital and the car park. Wonderful though our National Health Service is in so many ways, it's not renowned for the catering. If I was to provide a sandwich for the birth of my son, it would be the finest sandwich I could lay my hands on.

A Sainsbury's supermarket was up the road. And not just any Sainsbury's – this was their flagship store with a grass roof and everything. The stars had aligned that day. They would offer an array of sandwiches like no other. I pulled into the car park and brought the car to a stop in the middle of a parent-and-child space. I knew technically *I wasn't* and, technically, *he wasn't* either – at least, not yet – but if ever I felt justified in parking there, it was that day.

I wanted someone to stop me. To dare challenge me so that I could fix them with a steely-eyed glare and bellow in my most masculine voice, 'I-DON'T-HAVE-TIME-FOR-THIS! MY-WIFE-IS-IN-LABOUR-AND-I...' (at this point I would turn away from them, maybe throw in a little flounce and then stride purposefully towards the store doors) 'I HAVE-A-MISSION!'

No one said anything. I shuffled quietly to the entrance, took a basket and went to peruse the sandwich aisle. I thought back to the Aussies and their self-help books. They'd mentioned packing some nuts and raisins together with a favourite drink, but not a single one of them explained the hidden meaning behind someone in labour saying that they don't mind which sandwich you choose for them. Does it mean the pain is so unbearable they just want something plain? Or does it mean that they really crave something more exotic but they don't like to say as they don't want to come across as a burden? You can see the dilemma I faced that day. And all along my wife is lying in the bed up the road, oblivious to it all.

In the end I opted for a selection of sandwiches. A veritable buffet, carefully selected from the 'Taste the Difference' luxury range. *Only the best for you, my son.*

Crisps! We would need crisps to go with the sandwiches. I shunned the Hula Hoops and Quavers; they didn't have the gravitas the situation demanded. Kettle Chips. Salt and black pepper. We would dine on Kettle Chips at the birth of our first child. And a packet of pickled onion Space Invaders for the drive back to the hospital.

Fruit. She'd want fruit after all that savouriness. I silently

congratulated myself as I considered the selection. A lesser husband and dad-to-be wouldn't be so thoughtful. They wouldn't
consider taking back a palate cleanser. As I put a fruit salad and
some grapes into the basket I reminded myself just what a lucky
wife she was. Drinks. Of course, drinks. Still or sparking? I'd
better get both, just in case.

Twenty-nine pounds I spent in Sainsbury's that day. I strode
back into the hospital, my three brimming, orange carrier bags
swinging freely by my side. I walked with the swagger and
importance of someone delivering a heart to the transplant
ward. It would all be OK. Man. Provider. He had returned.

'I DON'T WANT A F*CKING SANDWICH, I WANT
THIS THING OUT OF ME!!!!' were the words that greeted
me. I slumped back into the chair in the corner of the room, out
of the way where I belonged.

It was another twenty-five hours that my wife spent in labour.
For all the talk around which sex suffers the greater burdens in
life, there's not a single word spoken that isn't silenced by the
actions that each and every mother takes simply to give the gift
of life. And her reward that day for giving every part of herself?
She was to lie there, drained and exhausted, as her pride and joy
was handed to the sobbing buffoon sitting in the corner, smelling
of pickled onion Space Invaders.

And son, one day when you read this I want you to know
that all those thoughts of ever wanting a girl melted away the
minute I held you. From that first moment, I realized that all I
ever wanted… was you. And I'd like to tell you that in those first

precious moments of life, we looked into each other's eyes and that your dad leant down and whispered something profound and meaningful that we will both carry with us for the rest of our days. I'd like to tell you that, but I can't. Because the minute you were put in my arms, I panicked. 'He's too perfect,' I thought. 'He's too good. Look at him. I'll just mess it all up.'

And although the years have rolled away since that moment, I don't really think that feeling ever has.

CHAPTER THREE

Build

And so we took you home. And the light, it skipped and shone off those glasses with a rose tint that your dad wore every time he looked at you. Then that little baby started to grow, up and out into the world. Then people started whispering, 'Shouldn't he be talking by now?' 'Shouldn't he be walking by now?' But what did they know? They were comparing him to everyone else, but you couldn't compare him to anyone else, because everyone else was only ever like that fake diamanté stuff from a TV shopping channel, but this boy… This boy was the Koh-i-Noor.

MY SON'S NOT RAINMAN BLOG

S ome people are natural parents. Instinct kicks in – they just know what to do. Looking back, I'm not sure either of us were. His mum was certainly better at it all than me. I remember the midwife leaving us to dress him for the first time in a baby grow. We were terrified. Even though the midwife was horrible and rude and bossy, I wanted her to come home and live with us forever because she knew how this all worked.

The trouble was, I'd never really held anything so fragile before. At least, not since I was seven years old and my brothers and I found a dying magpie lying in the road and decided the best course of action was to bring it home, put it in a cardboard box with some bread and milk, and watch it slowly die, much to the delight of my mother. I remember how small and frail that magpie seemed, but even then nobody asked me to put it in a bloody cardigan. You see that was the problem with The Boy; at any point I thought I was going to snap him. There wasn't a chapter on how-to-bend-an-arm-that-won't-move-into-a-ba-by-grow-so-you-don't-smash-it-into-a-thousand-little-pieces in any of the baby books. Too basic even by their standards. I'd even done the prenatal course. Me and lovely Dwayne the carpet fitter (the only other bloke who turned up) had a practice with a doll, but at least a doll's arm moved when you wanted it to. They prepare you for the head being fragile; all the books mention how delicate the skin is on their head. But how come no one mentioned the neck? The neck was next to useless – the head would have been fine if it had a decent neck to sit itself on in the first place.

Every time I picked up The Boy I just felt clumsy and awkward. I thought parenting was going to be all storytelling and puppet shows and finger painting but it wasn't, not in those early days. To begin with it was practical. I've never even put up a shelf before, I still can't tell my left from right properly and I can't use a tin opener. I tried to be hands-on, but it soon became apparent that I couldn't even put a nappy on properly. I never secured the fastener tightly enough because I thought I might smash his pelvic bone into smithereens. Parenting, it just never came naturally in those early days.

And I had good reason for feeling clumsy. I'm renowned for it. I can't carry a cup of coffee across a room without spilling half of it on the floor, so how on earth was I meant to manage with a living, breathing child? As our families excitedly arrived at the hospital to come and visit the new arrival, whenever I went to pick him up I'd hear a collective gasp from whoever was around the bed at the time. Instinctively, people would just cry out in unison, 'Watch his head, John.'

'He's fine,' I'd reassure them, his ear narrowly missing the edges of the bedside cot as I desperately tried to make it all look as natural as possible. It was a constant reminder that I was responsible for someone else now. And I'd do it right. I should have known that was easier said than done.

The next day it was time to take my son ('My son' – every time I uttered those words my heart swelled) and his exhausted mum home. I arrived on the maternity ward on a boiling hot day in April, wearing my thickest coat that I couldn't take off as

I hadn't ironed any of my clothes and without a belt to keep the trousers where they should be.

'Have you got any pound coins for parking?' I said to his exhausted mum who was sitting patiently on a ready-made bed, belongings packed, son in her arms. 'I forgot to bring my wallet…'

There was something profound about the journey home from hospital that I hadn't been expecting. In the hospital none of it had quite seemed real. If we were unsure of anything, a midwife was a call-button away or there was always someone visiting. Yet suddenly here we were, alone in it all. Mum sitting in the back seat outwardly calm, her nervousness betrayed by her white knuckles visible as she clasped both sides of his car seat tightly, as if this oh-most-precious cargo might spontaneously combust at any point. As I started the car I adjusted the rear-view mirror to ensure I had a clear view of his face and we slowly moved off. The outside world fell away and for the first time it was just the three of us. A family.

I'd never realized just how many potholes there were in south-east London until that journey home. Then there were the speed bumps, protruding out of the tarmac like giant baby killers. Don't they know he's got no neck! The roads were a disgrace. Other people were a disgrace, driving too fast, taking risks, clogging up the streets with unnecessary journeys. Had no one spotted the 'Baby on board' sticker I proudly attached to the rear window last night? The only time I've ever driven so carefully since was when driving home from a speed-awareness course. The car never got out of second gear the entire way.

Of course, I'd heard him cry on the hospital ward. It seemed almost cute there, this gentle wailing against the backdrop of other babies, people coming and going and the general business of the hospital. It was barely audible, tiny little lungs desperate to leave their mark on the world. Now, within the confines of our small London flat with its paper-thin walls, he showed exactly what he was capable of.

There's something about your own child's cries. They're broadcast on a different wavelength to those of other children. You could be in a room of two hundred babies all wailing their hearts out and pick yours out in an instant. As a parent, it's a skill that never leaves you. I've sat in soft-play centres and heard the cry from afar and, like Tarzan, Lord of the Jungle, I've known it's for me. I've been pulled into schools and heard the same faint noise from the far end of a playing field. And it's only writing it down now that I realize how much that saddens me: how much he has cried over the years in order to be heard.

Those first few weeks at home were tough. There were moments where it felt like the crying might never stop. A few years ago I was on a child development course for a job I had at the time and one of the talks was about attachment theory, how the bond formed in the early months of life is so important to a child's future development. It described how neglect is often more harmful than abuse to the long-term outcome for a person, since at least abuse is some form of contact. Chilling. It talked about how maybe our generation got it wrong. In the seventies you had a 'good baby' if they didn't cry, made no noise and could generally be left for hours on their own. But crying is a baby's only form of communication. And a baby soon learns to stop crying if no one comes.

I might be reading too much into all this now, but I was never sure where a baby like ours fitted in with all this. Here was a baby who cried and cried and, despite our best intentions as parents, we never seemed able to meet his needs because we never seemed to discover what they were. Sometimes it felt like he just wasn't pleased to be here very much.

That makes it all sound awful and of course it wasn't. It might well have been a perfectly normal start to life. I hope that by now you're beginning to recognize that I have a habit of over-thinking and over-analysing everything. I've only had the one experience of having a baby and bringing up a child. Much like I'm his only experience of having a father. It's all each of us know. Now there's a terrifying thought.

So life went on, and we relaxed into our new roles a little bit more. I remember our first trip out as a family, a fortnight after we came home from the hospital. I was due to return to work after the weekend, so we thought we'd do our first family outing to Bluewater shopping centre, just east of London. It might seem like it was a random choice, but it was selected for a number of reasons:

1   Fairly close by with minimal speed bumps and a very sensible 50mph speed limit on the main roads.
2   Indoors to protect the newborn baby from the dangers of air.
3   Baby-changing facilities.
4   If anything was forgotten, it could be purchased at Bluewater.
5   What else can you do with a baby?

That morning, my wife piled up the entire contents of the flat at the door and I loaded it into the car. We got the car seat attached in only forty-seven minutes, knocking a good four minutes off the previous personal best on leaving the hospital; we were getting so much better at all this. That was it, we were off. After a gentle drive during which I twice allowed myself to cruise in third gear, we arrived at Bluewater. I reversed into the parent-and-child bay feeling warm and smug. As I stepped out of the car, I half expected the world's paparazzi to swarm around us. Here I am, everyone, a virile father with his family.

And off we went, my wife pushing the pushchair, me carrying the contents of our home in a rucksack. We headed into Bluewater and it was perfect. He slept the whole time, we went for a coffee, the ambient temperature was to everyone's satisfaction, the trip was great. We were doing it, this parenting thing. We'd forgotten nothing, our son was safe, we were just like everyone else. We headed back to the car park, congratulating ourselves on a perfect day out, being perfect parents (I say day, it was

an hour and a half). We'd do it more often, this going out business, it was easy. At first I couldn't remember where I'd parked
the car, but then I saw it from a distance. It was pretty easy to
spot, really; it was the one with both rear doors wide open and
the keys in the boot, just the way we'd left it. Perfect parents.

It's funny, the transition from the neuroticism of the early
days of parenting to the nonchalance that soon kicks in. I'm
not really sure when it happened, but it did and quite quickly.
The rucksack was soon replaced with a nappy and a few wipes
shoved in a pocket. I saw other 'Baby on board' stickers and
realized most of them were on Volvos and quietly removed my
own. And eventually I stopped waiting for strangers to stop me
in the street and tell me that they've done a survey and, although
everybody says it, mine genuinely was by far the most beautiful
baby that they've ever seen.

People ask now if there were 'any signs' in those early weeks.
I don't know. I don't know what we should have been looking
for even if we were looking for it. I had nothing to compare him
to. The crying continued, I know that much. Early evening and
then into the night. His mum bore the brunt of it. I remember
walking home from the train station after work, Tarzan hearing
the cry from up the road and then walking around the block
one more time before I could bring myself to face it. My poor
wife, exhausted at the door.

'I'm sure it's just a bit of colic,' the health visitor repeated
whenever the subject was raised. 'Don't worry, he'll grow out
of it.'

Oh, son, how I wish we could have helped you more.

In those early months my contribution always seemed to be in the kitchen as it's fair to say that my wife wasn't a great cook. As a result, I did most of the cooking at home. And most of the eating. I remember when we were dating I was promised a sample of her 'special recipe'. (Reading that line back has made me laugh. Part of me thinks I should delete it, but the schoolboy in me wants it to stay. It's staying.) Her special recipe was Boston baked beans. For weeks I was promised this culinary delight, the recipe a secret that had been handed down from the forefathers of Boston itself or something like that. It turned out Boston baked beans was baked beans with some treacle in it and it was as hideous as it sounds. That was the last time she cooked, until her son arrived.

I came home from work one day and, as well as the customary crying, there was something new to greet me: smells wafting from the kitchen, lovely cooking smells. Ah, dinner, I foolishly thought to myself. I popped my head around the door; it was an impressive sight. Blender out, pans out and on the work surface lots of ice cube trays filled with colourful dollops of puree.

'What's this?' I asked.

'Don't come in here without washing your hands!' She rattled through each ice cube tray. 'This is organic sweet potato and butternut squash. This is fennel, artichoke and some other vegetable I've never even heard of. This is apple and pear compote...' The Boy would dine like a king on his first solids. That night, I gave him his bath, put him to bed and phoned for a takeaway.

Maybe I've painted the wrong picture here. A pair of neurotic parents with a screaming baby – it's as if a psychiatrist would have a field day. I suppose the sad thing is that the crying and the unsettled behaviour in the evening has taken over as the main memory. But it certainly wasn't the only one. The Boy could smile. He had a smile that you could dine out on for weeks. Other people debated about whether it was really a smile or just a bit of wind, but it didn't matter. All that mattered was that those precious moments were enough to get us through the relentless sleepless nights.

And it wouldn't be long before that smile turned into a laugh. A laugh that had a life of its own, that would gargle and chuckle and forever march to a different beat. When I look back now, I realize that in those first few weeks of his life he taught me more about myself and the so-called meaning of life than anyone has before or since. Before he came along, I thought I was a nice person. I thought I did things for others because I was good or kind. Only now do I recognize that so often I did things for others because I wanted something in return, be it praise or thanks. But in those precious first weeks he taught me what it means to truly love someone. To give everything and expect nothing in return; maybe that's the true definition of love.

CHAPTER FOUR

A Family Affair

There's something strangely hypnotic about watching your own child sleeping. I've found myself doing it often over the years, going into his room to quickly say goodnight and, before I know it, I've been there for minutes, even hours, just silently studying him, learning him. Over time, the surroundings might have changed – from the glow of a nightlight and the chimes of a long-forgotten nursery rhyme to the flickering screen of a left-on iPad and the shouts and clashes of a far-off Power Ranger, but the serenity, the calmness on his face, they have largely stayed the same.

Whatever drama and chaos may have dominated during the waking hours, they have always seemed a distant memory as he sleeps. No furrowed brow, no sign of anxiety, just a little boy at peace with himself and the world.

And then, in a few hours' time, he'll waken. There'll be no snooze button, no five more minutes. The Boy's eyes have always sprung open from sleep with an urgency that wasn't always appreciated in the adjacent bedroom. Looking back, I suppose it's one of the most defining moments of being a child. He opens his eyes, flings the bedcovers to one side and leaps out of bed. There's no doubt about it, today is *the* day. There is a world to be discovered, and a life to be lived. Each and every morning, etched on his face is the undeniable knowledge that today, this very day, is going to be the best day of his life. EVER. It doesn't matter what day it is, it could even be a Monday, but it will always, without fail, be the best day.

When do we lose that?

MY SON'S NOT RAINMAN BLOG

They were quite isolating I suppose, those first twelve months of The Boy's life. We were the first of our friends to have children and both of our families lived hundreds of miles away. We were fortunate to have my younger brother nearby and he very soon adapted to his new role in life of Best Uncle Ever, a title he's never really lost. At that time he had no children of his own, but he was a natural parent and was always tuned into The Boy's wavelength in a way that others could only hope to replicate.

We'd travel to see the rest of our families too – in North Wales or Scotland. And they'd travel down to London to visit us. It was always lovely to see them, my heart swelling with pride as they cooed over The Boy in whatever new bought-for-the-occasion outfit he was wearing at the time. Hasn't he grown! Doesn't he look like both of you! Hasn't his hair got lighter!

And then a few hours into the visit, when they'd had time to settle and it became clearer that The Boy wasn't quite meeting whatever developmental milestone we should have reached by that time – sitting up or crawling or making sounds – someone would invariably offer their own parenting advice or opinion they believed might make all the difference. Often it felt like the opinion was that he was pampered too much – just leave him be, let him cry, he'll soon stop. Put the toy out of his reach, he'll grab for it eventually.

I understand now that all this was done from a place of love and I even catch myself doing it unintentionally nowadays when I visit new parents. How soon we forget what it was to know nothing about newborn babies and just allow instinct to carry us through. Every generation seems to feel like the next are too spoilt, too cared for, dare we say it, *too loved*?

That sounds almost too cruel a description of the friends and family I love dearly, especially when I know they just wanted to offer some reassurance. Everything was OK, they'd say. Your brother didn't walk until he was twenty months; your grandmother's sister cried non-stop until her twenty first birthday… Maybe my memory of those events says more about my own insecurities at the time than anything else. Sometimes it just felt like they were only serving to highlight my own shortcomings.

I was more likely to win Rear of the Year than Dad of the Year, I knew that, but we were doing our best.

I think that was the toughest part of that stage – there was no diagnosis to back things up. I had an instinct that something *might* not be quite right, but nothing I could really put my finger on. There was just a whole group of people whose love clouded their judgement, who didn't want to accept that anything might be wrong. Instead, they over-compensated, looked for other reasons to explain what was going on. And invariably that would occasionally mean pointing the finger at the two amateur parents in the middle of it all.

I can remember when I heard the *a* word mentioned for the first time. Autism. Much like imagining a world without my child in it, it seems strange now to imagine a world in which I never really knew what it was, where it was just another condition that didn't really affect me so I blithely ignored it.

It was one of my brothers who first said the word. He was my twin and a head teacher. We all had children around the same time – my elder brother already had two children, then within twelve months along came The Boy, swiftly followed a few weeks later by my twin's son with a brilliant shock of red hair and personality to match. The Boy Who Loves Being Ginger had arrived in the world – poor Nana would have to wait another few years for her elusive granddaughter.

I suppose there was a certain inevitability to the cousins' friendship, given that their dads are twin brothers, and the closeness in age, yet it's funny how different they seemed as babies.

The Boy Who Loves Being Ginger's developmental milestones seemed to just be targets to be beaten, a checklist to tick off so the family could get on with the very real business of living. The Boy seemed more passive, I suppose. He'd get there eventually, when he wanted to, but he'd just take his time.

If anything he came across as distracted and ill at ease with the world. It's difficult looking back now, with the knowledge I've gained over the years, because at the time I knew none of that stuff and, if I had, maybe I would have spotted things sooner. But everything seemed so easily explained. The excessive dribbling was because he was teething or liked putting things in his mouth; he didn't crawl because some babies don't, he'll go straight to walking; he's stubborn, his mum was the same as a baby.

Yes, I had a sense my son was different, but in comparison to my brothers I had also been different. When we were growing up, they were the cool ones, they were the ones that were forever begging me to play football with them so they could have a goalkeeper, they were the ones with the first detentions and the first ones with girlfriends. I was the quiet, withdrawn one, the one who spent all his time in his bedroom reading and daydreaming. I can't catch a ball, I still struggle with shoelaces, I didn't even discover that you sat on the toilet seat and not on the rim until I was nineteen years old. I suppose I just put the differences The Boy showed in those early years down to me. He was different because I was different – anything that appeared out of the ordinary was just down to being 'son of John'.

It happened when we were in my brother's car, I guess with
The Boy around the age of two. I'm not sure where we'd been,
but we'd put the two children into their car seats in the back.
The respective dads reached in through each passenger door
to fasten the kids' seat belts. The Boy Who Loves Being Ginger
had already fastened his. Even at that age, he had a streak of
independence, a desire and a thirst to do things alone. By the
age of four he would be out gardening and tending to the lawn.
The Boy wasn't even an arm's length away from him in the car
but at that very moment it seemed like he was a whole world
apart. I don't think The Boy had even noticed a seatbelt, let
alone worked out how to pull it around himself. It's something
he struggles with to this day. He'd never move out of the way to
help or lean over slightly so you could slot the belt together. It
was always as if it was happening for the first time. I suppose if
there was any sign early on, it was this lack of inquisitiveness,
the lack of wanting to know or to learn that seems to fill most
children's every waking moment.

I got into the front seat of the car, my brother next to me.
I noticed him continuously looking in the rear-view mirror
at the two boys sitting side-by-side, only weeks separating
them in age. The Boy Who Loves Being Ginger was peering
round his dad's seat, eager to see the control panel light up as
the engine started. The Boy was next to him, perfectly happy
in his own little world, dribbling away to his heart's content,
chewing on the delectable seat belt that had just been served
as a light snack.

'John, do you think he might be autistic?' he asked me.

Fuck. Off. I'm not really one for displays of anger but I remember the rage that filled me that day. You may have noticed that I used the f-word a couple of chapters ago but I asterisked one of the letters out to make it more polite. This one's staying in. I'm not sure why the comment upset me so much. Maybe it was the bluntness of the word. He didn't say, 'Do you think something might be wrong?' He just came out with it. Autism. I suppose it felt like rejection, this idea that there might be something wrong with my son. Because that's what autism means, isn't it? Was I really that shallow?

We all want people to love our children. We want people to tell us that they're the most beautiful, the most intelligent, the most advanced. And, in some messed-up way, it felt like my brother was saying he didn't love him. If he thought there was something wrong with him, how could he love him? He was perfect, wasn't he, my boy?

It was unfair to my brother to think that. There was always going to be someone who would say the word first and it just happened to be him. Maybe I felt it should have been me, in my role as parent. I should have been the one to speak the seemingly unspeakable. We drove back to his house in silence. This new word, 'autism', that I'd barely even known moments earlier, now hung in the air like the fragrance of a cheap, crappy air freshener. I returned home and fired up the computer.

Ten minutes later, Windows 98 burst into life. I dialled the Internet connection, the reassuring buzz of the line temporarily drowning out the noise in the background as my wife tried to settle my son for the night. I opened up AltaVista and I typed those six letters on the keyboard. A-U-T-I-S-M. Seeing the word appear across the screen for the first time, I hit search.

CHAPTER FIVE

Lesson One

Today The Boy is unwell. It's not a regular occurrence really. It starts in the night, a barbaric yelp in the dark at two in the morning. I rush into his bedroom, standing on the obligatory piece of Lego en route just to ensure I am in fully sympathetic mode by the time I reach his bedside. He is all scrunched up in bed, pulling his knees into his chest.

'My waist,' he howls. 'My waist really hurts a little bit.'

Now, I'm no medical expert, but I'm guessing if I phone NHS Direct with the symptoms 'It really hurts a little bit', they too might well be stumped. However, the screams into the night suggest the pain might be closer aligned to the 'really' part of the sentence than the 'little bit'. *Never fear, son, the doctor will see you now. I shall investigate further.*

I know from past experience that I am only awarded three

questions to get to the root of the problem. Any more and the additional pressure of having to answer questions he doesn't know the answer to will cause a meltdown to accompany the deathly screams we are currently experiencing. I break it down into simple, easy-to-manage sentences. Once again this boy – who can speak so well about subjects that mean so little – can't find the words to express himself when it really matters.

'Show Daddy where it hurts.'

'Everywhere!' he screams, clutching himself tighter.

'Is it inside or outside?'

'Both!' his voice going up an octave to remind me I only have one more question left before we go to that place we don't want to go.

I offer the solution I always offer. The only thing I know.

'Let's try to go to the toilet.'

And off we hobble to the bathroom, the change of scenery, the cold tiles under bare feet helping to calm him. The pain still comes in waves, but quieter now. He's going to live.

So we're off school today. He still has pains in his stomach. I think. And that's just it – I think. It's just guesswork. I'm still none the wiser as to what's wrong. Everything manifests itself as pain in the stomach for him. Anxiety, stress, depression, appendicitis – all have the same symptoms. And they just serve as a reminder that, despite his fluency, the words just won't come when it really matters. This boy who can talk until the end of time itself about how to make a diamond pick axe in *Minecraft* can't find the words to tell someone he's hurting.

And that makes me really sad a little bit.

N ow, settle down class. It feels like this should be the part of the book where I offer up the definitive answer to 'What is autism?' I will enlighten you with my wit and wisdom as I describe perfectly the condition and how it affects those with the diagnosis. (Worldwide diagnosis rates vary hugely. Currently, it's estimated there are 1 in 100 people in the UK, and as many as 1 in 68 in the US.) Except I just can't do it.

Apparently the family have lived with autism for coming up to thirteen years now, but I don't know if I'm any closer to defining the condition than I was when I first typed the word into that ageing computer all those years ago. Each and every day The Boy continues to baffle, amaze, frustrate and confuse me in equal measure. And that's just the way things should be. I can't describe autism to you as if I'm some sort of expert, because all I know is *his* story. He no more represents every autistic person than I represent every middle-aged man with green eyes. If I've become an expert on anything over the years, it's him. Just him. And even he evades me most of the time.

The Internet is a strange and mystical place where you can find pretty much anything if you want to. Fancy finding a link between the speed of toenail growth and the likelihood of a cardiac arrest before the age of forty? Search for long enough and it's there. The same applies to autism – enter the behaviour that is of concern and soon enough you will have documented proof that there exists a link between that and autism. I'd like to tell you that when I read the search results ten years ago as they tumbled on to the screen, it felt like someone was describing my son perfectly. It didn't. And in so many ways it still doesn't.

Much of what I read didn't match my son at all. The repetitive body movements, an intense interest in certain objects, the lining up of toy cars. He was more likely to smash a toy car to pieces than place it in a perfect line with others. For each of the criteria he seemed to meet there were another two he didn't. Maybe if things had been more straightforward we'd have pushed for more help earlier. I'm not a clinician or researcher, I'm just a parent, but in many ways the term 'autism' seemed to be an umbrella term to describe a range of conditions that didn't always fit elsewhere. As an educational psychologist once said to me, 'Show me a child with autism and I'll show you a child.' (Don't worry, you're not alone, I thought she was a smart arse too.)

I guess this is where I'm putting in a kind of health warning. If you've picked up this book thinking that you're going to better understand autism, then I'm not sure it's right for you. All I can ever share with you is the story of one boy. There will be behaviour that might just be that exhibited by a little boy just doing as little boys do; some of it might be the result of autism; some of it may be the cerebral palsy that was diagnosed further down the line, and some of it will be a result of the unique conglomerate of cells that is The Boy.

But how much is age, how much autism, how much upbringing, how much cerebral palsy, how much personality? I used to think of autism in terms of an impenetrable cloak that surrounded him and if I could just discover how to remove it there would be this 'cured' being on the inside. But over the years I've learnt there isn't any one point where the autism ends and he begins. He's just him. And that's the way it should be.

So there may well be behaviours and situations that people can relate to but I'm afraid that's about as good as it gets in terms of my being able to describe the condition. Just as an example, it's estimated that over twenty-five per cent or one in four of all people with autism have no or very limited speech. Twenty-five per cent. Another huge percentage of those with autism have associated learning difficulties. There are people who will need a lifetime of support, while alongside those are some who are savants, with incredible skills and memory (who coincidentally might also need a lifetime of support).

This story I'm telling of The Boy can't possibly represent everyone's journey, no matter how much I'd love it to. That's why I said earlier that this isn't really even a book about autism. It's just the story of one boy, told through the eyes of one man. That's all it can ever be. I'm not sure how useful it will be in years to come to continue to have one word to describe such a cross-section of society. In forty years' time maybe the term autism won't exist, much as the term used to described it fifty years ago, 'childhood schizophrenia', doesn't exist now.

There was one behaviour that never appeared on the 'How to tell if your child has autism' checklists. Yet, as well as the dribbling and the slight speech delay, it's probably been the thing that has defined autism for us as a family over the years. And that behaviour is biting.

That's right, The Boy is – and has been ever since he procured his first tooth – a biter. Maybe one of the least attractive (if that's even the right way of thinking about it) of the autistic traits. He doesn't just bite other children – he's fairly indiscriminate in that sense – he'll go for anyone. Joking aside, it's a behaviour that The Boy dislikes immensely and I've struggled about including it in the book because of that. But I feel I can't tell his story without it, since it's what has caused us the most difficulties.

It's the behaviour that has led to exclusion after exclusion from childminders, nurseries, after-school clubs, mainstream schools and even special schools. Yet still it's a behaviour that people don't often talk about. Given its prevalence you will probably find information about biting on the websites of most autism charities, but it will never be on the front page. It's like the unacceptable face of autism that must be kept hidden behind closed doors. When autism is talked about in the media, it is too often discussed in terms of 'quirkiness' and even of being 'just a bit nerdy' like that bloke off *The Big Bang Theory*.

There will be a young boy (it's always an autistic boy on the telly, the ever-increasing number of girls being diagnosed seem to never get a look in), and he'll be around the age of six or seven. He'll be a very solitary child, who doesn't like mixing with others. He'll prefer to spend his days sitting alone in the corner of the room, facing the wall, reading train timetables. He'll sit his maths GCSE around the age of eight and three quarters, learn to play grade eight piano by the time he's eleven, sit A-level advanced physics at the age of thirteen, and in between he'll just fill his time memorizing the phone book. Well, there's another side to autism that isn't mentioned enough: incredibly difficult behaviours, behaviours that cause harm to both the individual and those around them.

Does every person with autism present with challenging behaviour? Certainly not, but there are many that do. Those behaviours can vary enormously, from physical aggression (such as biting) and self-injury (such as banging their own head on the walls and the floor), through to smearing (the commonly used term for smearing excrement on walls and furniture). It's difficult to comprehend, but right now there are still many men and women (and in some instances children) with autism and/or associated learning disabilities who are being held in hospitals and institutions around the world because they are deemed to be at such a high risk of harming both themselves and those around them. That's the reality of autism for some families. Yet if we don't talk about it those people are in danger of being kept hidden away from society for years to come. Through openness comes understanding and through understanding comes change.

The reasons for challenging behaviour can be as complex and varied as the condition itself. Sensory issues, anxiety, frustration and sometimes just learned behaviour all play their part and trying to unpick these effects can take years.

I think, certainly here in the UK, we're getting better at recognizing challenging behaviour as a form of communication (most schools will nowadays chant back the mantra 'all behaviour is communication' in meetings), but applying that knowledge to the everyday seems to be a difficult process. Take biting as an example. If you have communication difficulties and don't feel you can always get yourself heard, in many ways biting is the perfect solution.

Let's say you're at preschool and you've just had the time of your life in the sandpit. Later in the afternoon, if you play your cards right, you may well dabble in a spot of finger-painting. You don't really have a care in the world. But first, it's snack time. Time to munch away on twelve raisins stored in a box that is the perfect size to store twelve raisins. And when raisin number seven puts up a fight and refuses to budge out of the box, your fingers are just the right size to pluck him out of there. There's a contentment to the world. Just being alive, in the here and now, three years of age, there's no finer place to be. Then you look up and across the table sits Shane.

You've been coming to this place with Shane for a while now, and he's always sitting across the table. But today Shane has put down his raisins. He's discovered something far more important to fill his time than a snack of dried fruit. Shane is a maverick who chooses not to live by the nursery rules. Or he's just forgotten they existed and is so carried away with the joy of the moment that nothing else matters; it's difficult to say. Either way, Shane has disregarded the No Toys Allowed At The Snack Table rule and is pushing a toy car back and forth along the table top.

You discard your raisins. Any sense of hunger or enjoyment from eating has vanished. Your eyes are just drawn to that small, orange car. Mesmerized, you watch it going back and forth in Shane's hand, gliding along the table top. Each turn of the small rubber wheels takes you further and further into your hypnotic trance. Seconds earlier you didn't even know that car existed but now, right now, you know your life will never be complete without that orange car in your hand. You want it. More than you've wanted anything for at least twelve minutes. And this is where the problems start. Because you want that car more than anything in the entire universe. But Shane has the car. It's Shane's car. But you really, really want the car. And you can't find the words inside yourself to ask Shane for the car. Without even thinking, a solution comes to you. If you can't find the words, there is another way you can get the car. You lean across the table and sink your teeth into Shane's arm. Shane makes a yelping noise, but you ignore that. Like magic, his hand releases its hold on the car. Perfect, job done. You have the car. Thanks, Shane.

And once biting works for you in one way, it starts to work in lots of other ways too. There are so many things The Boy struggles with – day-to-day sounds, noise, lights can all become too much – as if he has a heightened sensitivity to it all. Ever since he was born he has regarded the vacuum cleaner as a mobile torture unit. The noise it made was unbearable for him. It's like he experiences the world on a different frequency and everything is intensified. And when it all becomes too much, when the sensory overload reaches fever pitch and he feels he might explode as the turmoil rages and builds inside him, sinking his teeth into something soft is a release. All that tension, that built up fear and anger inside of him, is released.

And writing this now makes me come across as some kind of super parent. Ooh, isn't he brilliant to have such insight into his son's mind? But really, I'm a fraud. It's taken years to get to this point. Years of dragging him around soft-play centres, with their bright lights, screaming children and activity, and wondering why he always hit out when anyone came near him. Years to finally understand just what he was trying to tell me. If indeed all behaviour is communication, then for years I didn't listen. It wasn't because I didn't want to, it was because I didn't know how to. I couldn't grasp that someone with the power of speech couldn't use it to express their basic needs and desires.

When I typed the word 'autism' into the computer that night after returning from my brother's house, it just didn't seem to match, probably because I didn't want it to. Son of John was just a few months behind his peers, that was all.

I'm sorry I didn't have the answers, son. For so long, I'm not even sure I understood what the questions were.

CHAPTER SIX

Distant Relatives

Sometimes in life we can't avoid trauma. Sometimes we just have to face the things we fear the most and deal with them. We know it will be hard, but through adversity comes strength. When we face our fears, we overcome anything.

Today was Haircut Day.

I have managed to keep Haircut Day to a biannual affair. There was one year when I felt particularly brave and I took him quarterly. I couldn't do that now. I've lost the fight.

There's a fine balance between hair-cutting and letting it grow. If there's one thing The Boy hates just as much as Haircut Day, it's Hair-Wash Day. And sadly Hair-Wash Day comes around a lot quicker. And the longer the hair, the longer Hair-Wash Day takes. It's a balancing act.

Now, I have been to most barbers in the south-east London

area with The Boy over the last ten years. Most of them we only visit once. The battle scars for both cutter and cuttee have been too much.

'Why not cut his hair yourself?' I hear you cry. I did. Once. I'm sure I made my ex-wife cry many times during our marriage but nothing will compare to the tears she cried when she saw the results after I'd cut her son's hair. I think it was using nail scissors for the fringe that tipped her over the edge.

Now there is only one barber we go to. Nicholas, the Greek Cypriot. He is an old, gentle man who has been cutting hair for years. Nobody under the age of seventy goes near him. He is slapdash, has bad breath and is grumpy. He has no patience with children whatsoever. He is, however, the fastest barber I know. Oh and he's seven quid. And there's never a queue.

Nicholas reacts to the sight of me and The Boy like an illegal hot-dog seller might greet a Food Hygiene Inspector. Hiding his scowl, in one movement he removes The Boy's coat, whips out the gown and bundles The Boy into it like a straightjacket. Nicholas knows getting in there early is key. He gets The Boy in the chair and spins the chair away from the mirror so The Boy can look out of the window. We learnt four years ago not to bother with the mirror. Then Nicholas attacks with the scissors. The dexterity of this old man's fingers as the scissors dance over The Boy's hair leaves me stunned every time. As he goes he repeats constantly, 'Look at the big dog. Look at the big dog,' while gesturing through the window with his elbow. We have never seen the big dog.

The entire haircut lasts approximately three minutes. No water sprayed, no noisy clippers used. Nicholas is a good man. The Boy climbs down from the barber's chair and most of the hair that has been removed from his head is stuck to his face and neck with his own saliva. But he's smiling. The battle is over and he knows that Hair-Wash Day will be quicker than before.

Nicholas retires to the till in the corner, battle-weary but relieved that this day will be over for another six months. I hand him a tenner. He knows not to bother with the change. Danger money.

Me and The Boy leave through the door. 'I'm really good at getting my hair cut now, aren't I, Daddy?'

Yes, mate. You're just fine.

MY SON'S NOT RAINMAN BLOG

I've dropped The Boy off to spend time with his cousins – his favourite pastime by far – and I've come away again to do some writing.

I went on Airbnb and selected a self-contained cottage in North Wales. Oh, the exoticness. What it actually means is a lovely old dear has converted her garage into a bedsit. It's December and I can't begin to put into words how cold this place is. There's a thermostat on the wall for the central heating that is set to 12°C.

'Don't go mad with the heating, will you, love?' she said as she let me in. 'I don't charge a lot.' On the first day I snuck it up to thirteen but I went to the shops yesterday and when I came back I noticed that it'd been put back down. I sit here writing and not fifteen feet away across the garden is her conservatory, resplendent with flashing Christmas tree lights, the windows covered in condensation as her own central heating blasts full-on.

I hadn't realized just how emotional it is, going back in time. At every point I find myself suddenly sobbing over the bloody keyboard. Memories come flooding back, both good and bad. Beautiful moments of his childhood that were lost after the diagnosis. I suppose most of the sadness has come because I didn't understand him then as I do now. And if I had, maybe some things wouldn't have been quite such a struggle for him.

A few months passed after my brother first mentioned the *a* word. We'd put it to one side and carried on with life as best we could. I can't pretend it was far from our minds, both myself and his mum, especially as The Boy continued to stretch the timeline for his developmental targets to the absolute limits. But on each occasion, just as we were about to raise concerns, he'd confound us and come through. For example, walking – he'd eventually started to walk, precariously wobbling. There had been no build up to it, no real crawling – another milestone missed – instead we had a brilliant bit of bum-surfing and that was it, he was away. It felt like he was just living a life on his terms, not ours.

He had the strangest little walk on him though. Legs turned in, no real balance and his shins and knees were forever covered in bruises, each one testament to a fall. We weren't overly concerned – much like everything else, we simply thought he'd catch up one day. We mentioned it to the GP.

'He has knock-knees,' he reassured us. 'He'll grow out of it by the age of six or seven.' We had no reason to doubt things: he was doing everything *eventually*. We had concerns around The Boy's behaviour certainly, but that was put down to the 'terrible twos'. He was a toddler, he'd grow out of this too, right?

Once The Boy started nursery, it became clear how difficult he found transitioning from one event to another. It's something he continues to struggle with enormously to this day, that period where he must stop doing one task and start another. The morning routine was particularly difficult. It quickly became a skilled affair that required both parents. Every day it felt like playing with an old World War II bomb. It needed to be treated gently, carefully. It could go off at any point. Unlike a bomb, however, the worry was once The Boy went off he would continue to go off for the rest of the day.

We started to develop our own way of doing things. A sense of humour and the ability to turn every task into a game certainly helped. Years later after the diagnosis we would use little pictures stuck to doors and cupboards – visual reminders for The Boy to prepare him for what came next.

GET DRESSED > BREAKFAST > TELEVISION > BATHROOM > SHOES > GET OUT OF HERE

It is incredible just how much being able to visualize things helps him. But in those days there was none of that. Looking back I understand that each morning was like Groundhog Day for The Boy. He seemed to have no real memory of what happened the day before. As parents we knew what was coming next, as we'd done it all yesterday and the days that preceded that. But without a visual reminder for The Boy, there was no link. Each morning it seemed as though he was doing it all for the first time and his refusal to comply wasn't based on a 'toddler tantrum', as we thought, but rather came because everything was new and scary and he wanted it to stop. Eventually, we'd get there.

By far the most precarious stage, the one at which it could and so often did go horribly wrong, was the bathroom, even if the rest of the morning had gone relatively smoothly until this point. Teeth-brushing was a case in point. Or, to give it its full title, Hey, I'll Tell You What, Mate, We've Had Not a Bad Morning Getting Ready, How About We Head Into the Bathroom for a Fight? As with most things, with patience, practice and perseverance it became easier over the years. Different strategies have worked, some better than others. Musical toothbrushes, *Toy Story* toothbrushes, electric tooth-brushes, flashing toothbrushes and soft toothbrushes, they've all played their part. Strawberry toothpaste, banana toothpaste, bubble-gum toothpaste, you've served us well. Mint toothpaste, you will continue to be the root of all evil. Bicarbonate of soda toothpaste, you're beyond words.

Once teeth-brushing was complete (I say brushing, it was more just holding a toothbrush in his mouth for two minutes – it might as well have been a thermometer) we moved on to washing. To this day, we have to use ice-cold water. We never use the hot tap even to lightly warm the water – anything above freezing cold *burns* during the washing process. First The Boy puts his hands in the freezing water. He holds them there for longer than would appear humanly possible. On no account should his hands be rubbed together. Next he touches a bar of soap with the very tip of his fingers. That's the soap bit done. Now he throws water all down whatever clothes he is wearing that day. He is careful to avoid his face at all times.

Perfect. Face and hand washing done.

Every now and then things would go OK, as they do for every child. The Boy was nothing if not consistently inconsistent. It was on the days that the morning routine went really smoothly that we'd suddenly be lulled into a false sense of security and, like a fool, I'd reach for the hairbrush.

And so life went on. Each day The Boy eventually left for nursery with a mop of unkempt hair, water down his front and a smudge of toothpaste across his cheek.

Whatever struggles he had with the day-to-day routine of life, it was the monthly or bi-monthly events that caused him real anxiety. Take Toenail-Cutting Day, for example. Even now, ten years later, I still carry the battle scars from going into this one unprepared. He was around two years of age when we came up with the routine and it has largely remained unchanged. As for all great events, the key is in the preparation. Twenty-four hours is the optimal period to prepare The Boy for Toenail-Cutting Day. Any longer causes anxiety, any shorter and I might as well be performing open-heart surgery on him with a blunt teaspoon and no anaesthetic.

In order for Toenail-Cutting Day to have any hope of success we must follow these simple steps. Stage one:

Empty the bathroom of any items that aren't stuck down. Find the largest bath towel in the house and place it at the foot of the bath, ready. Put the nail scissors discreetly behind the toilet cistern, ready. It is of the utmost importance that these aren't spotted in advance. Lower the toilet seat lid. This will be the operating table.

Now we're ready for stage two:

Run the bath. Don't add any cold water. Only use boiling, almost scalding hot water. After calling, 'Bath's ready!', prepare for a ninety-minute battle to get The Boy into the bath, by which time the water will be at an ambient temperature. Now The Boy is in the bath he didn't want to get into, he will refuse to get out. Don't try to be clever and take the plug out. He will sit in a cold, empty bath quite happily. Instead, frighten him. Tell him that these horrible little creatures called bacteria live in the bath and they eat children's skin, starting at the fingertips and that's why they go all wrinkly. (Yes, I'm horrible, but needs must.)

As he leaps out of the bath wrap him in the large bath towel that was put in place earlier. Keep his arms tucked inside, that's key – imagine a roll of carpet with a head sticking out of one end and feet at the other. Still holding him, he can be lowered on to the toilet seat in the same movement – there should be just enough give in the towel for him to be bent into the sitting position. Now take out the nail scissors. Remember, speed is of the essence.

Now comes the weird bit. Each of the toenails has been assigned a name. The left foot is always girls, the right foot boys. The left big toe is always Fiona. On the right, it's Fred. The other names are allowed to change. And so the toenails are cut with phrases such as 'Oh, Florence, haven't you grown since I last saw you?' and 'Come on, Ted, be a good boy and get your haircut.' Sometimes… sometimes it's a blessing he bites his fingernails.

However, as bad as Haircut Day and Toenail-Cutting Day got, it was the nights that were the hardest. Even as a toddler, he raged and fought against going to sleep. It was starting to become obvious that The Boy hated being alone. It almost felt as if he might stop existing if someone wasn't with him. Constantly. We'd tried controlled crying, we'd tried wrapping him tightly. Nothing in those bloody self-help parenting books that still dominated the bookshelves seemed to work. It was exhausting, for all of us, not least The Boy. More often than not, I'd fall asleep lying with him as I read a bedtime story or his mum would. Without really even realizing it, she and I were spending less and less time together as a couple.

CHAPTER SEVEN

Scooby Dooby Doo

This morning I was woken at 6.10 a.m. by The Boy demanding an answer to the burning question, 'How old was God when He died?' I'm not sure what prompted this, but every answer I gave was wrong. I said He wasn't dead. The Boy asked where He was then. I said He was everywhere. The Boy said He can't be everywhere, He's not here. I said you can't see Him. The Boy said He's a ghost then. I said He's not a ghost, He's not dead. The Boy said where is He then...

IT'S SIX O'CLOCK IN THE MORNING ON A BANK HOLIDAY!

So I told him God died at the age of forty-eight – He finished building the world and then died. 'Is he in heaven?' Yes, yes, son, yes, I'm sure he is. Now please go and play in the road and leave me in bed for five more minutes.

It's not just God. Heaven was something we talked about a long time ago. Heaven is where Nosey and Fang the hamsters are, together with two great grannies, one grand-dad and a bird we found at the side of the road. We cried more tears for the bird than any of the others put together. They all live together in heaven and have a swimming pool. Everybody in heaven has a swimming pool. And XBox Live Gold.

I've told The Boy countless numbers of these shitty 'facts' over the years to make life easier. Most of them in the heat of the moment and then I've regretted them instantly. Later this year we're apparently going on holiday to Timbuktu because in 2009, in a moment of despair, I told him that's where the Power Rangers lived. But once you've said something, in his mind it becomes as real as he is. When he was younger he refused to wear a seatbelt. One day he took it off while I was driving along the motorway, and I told him that if you travelled in a car without a seatbelt on you would crash and die. That has now become set in stone. To this day, he will not let me start the car engine until everybody is securely strapped in and he has done a visual check. Until yesterday.

I pulled out of school and I didn't notice my seatbelt wasn't on. Neither of us did. The excitement of getting two Easter eggs from his teacher had distracted him. Fifty metres up the road I realized my error. I tried to pull the belt discreetly around me without him spotting it. I failed.

'I CAN'T BELIEVE YOU DIDN'T WEAR A SEATBELT AND NOW WE WILL DIE AND IT WILL BE YOUR FAULT. WHY DO YOU WANT TO KILL YOUR SON?!'

Tears were already streaming down his face, the rage filling every part of him, the fear all too real in his eyes.

'YOU'VE MADE ME REALLY ANGRY AND WHEN WE'VE DIED AND WE GET TO HEAVEN I'M GOING TO HIT YOU REALLY HARD FOR KILLING US.'

Yeah, look, about this heaven business...

MY SON'S NOT RAINMAN BLOG

'Hello, Mr Williams? Hello, it's Jane calling from the nursery. I was wondering if we could have a word.'

Ah, the infamous phone calls home. They started fairly quickly after he joined nursery and have remained a constant feature of his education. People sometimes have a perception of life with a special needs child – that, despite its difficulties, it's somehow a life of privilege with our own parking space, pushing in the front of the queue at Disneyland and getting to board the aircraft first. It creates an impression on the surface that all is well, that we as a society are doing our bit for our most vulnerable members and we can pat ourselves on the back and get on with our day. The reality of it, however, is a little different. Discreet phone calls, wanting a 'quick word'. 'Don't worry, it won't take long.'

The Boy was first removed from a nursery at the age of two and a half. It was accomplished in a more polite fashion, of course. An initial meeting. Concerns. He doesn't seem to be settling. He hasn't really made any friends. We'll keep an eye on him. Have we considered any other nurseries in the area? Maybe somewhere with a bit more space?

Then on to nursery number two. Once again, it's all smiles at first. We've made the right choice, they just couldn't get a handle on him at the old place. Look at his dimples! And freckles!! Isn't he lovely! Two weeks later he's described as a livewire. Another week and there's been an 'incident'. A phone call in the afternoon. Then one at lunchtime. Eventually we don't even make it to morning snack. Have you considered any other nurseries in the area? Maybe somewhere with an outdoor area?

Eventually, around the age of three and a half, we tried a childminder. We visited a few. Smaller groups, we thought, maybe he'd settle. Our first choice was lovely and I know she tried her best. She even let us down gently, although it has to be the first occasion where apparently the family cat has an allergy to a child rather than the other way around.

We both worked at this point, his mum and me. It seems easy to look back and think we should have given up work sooner. To be frank, we couldn't afford to. We didn't own our house, we were already living in one of the cheapest parts of London and money was incredibly tight. We just couldn't afford to drop to one wage.

Oh, what a miserable bloody picture I've painted. It wasn't a great time though. And I suppose what hurt the most was that with every phone call it felt as if here were people rejecting my child. *Rejecting him.* I touched on this earlier, I know, but let's face it, we all want our children to be loved and liked, to be popular. I never thought I was a particularly jealous person until that point. Jealousy is something we associate with jilted lovers or playground spats. We're so often told what a horrible emotion it is. And yet over the years it's one I've experienced time and time again, that has come back in waves, often when I least expect it. And even writing it down now, admitting it, seems to be some shameful confession: there were times when I was jealous of other people's children.

From strangers in the playground to my own beautiful nephews and niece, there were moments where I became jealous of them all. Every football goal scored, every exam passed, every joke told, they all caused this horrible feeling inside that I tried to push away. Why couldn't my son do that?

Thankfully the feeling has subsided over the years, but I still get over-emotional when people tell me what an amazing son I have. Because for so long no one ever did.

The one saving grace we had was to go home and visit family now and again. I can't pretend I didn't feel judged there as well, because I did feel it, even if that wasn't in reality the case. I had started to lose any confidence in myself as a parent. I thought, it must be something we did. Maybe we were too soft or too tough or not consistent enough. I just didn't know. And so he and I made plans to head away for a long bank holiday with his cousins. Mum would stay at home to give her a chance to catch her breath for a while.

We began by loading the car. By this point The Boy had started becoming very attached to things. Objects. I think they gave him a sense of security, a sense of consistency in an ever-changing world. The environment might change, but surrounding himself with familiar things helped to give him an anchor, a sense of self. He'd want to take things wherever we went. That caused all kinds of problems with the nursery because we weren't allowed to bring toys in, not since the day Shane had snuck in an orange car from home. Despite the staff seeing how distressed this rule made The Boy, they wouldn't budge. It only served to make that morning routine even more precarious.

We made preparations to travel up north, with The Boy having a few things he wanted to bring with him. I wheeled out his Winnie-the-Pooh suitcase and he knew instantly that meant we were going to visit his cousins. He selected a *Scooby-Doo* DVD to take with him. That would go in the suitcase. And seeing it in the suitcase all alone seemed to bring out his compassionate side. The poor, lonely DVD couldn't travel alone. It needed its friends. All the rest of his DVDs would go along as well. And now there was an issue. How could we take the DVDs without taking all the VHS videotapes too? They all belonged together. So every bit of recorded film we'd ever owned was put in the case. The suitcase was now overflowing. That was OK, we could just use the bed. And the last VHS videotape went on to the bed, *A Dinosaur's Tale.* Now it turned into a word association game. Dinosaurs. We needed to take his dinosaurs. All of them. Out came every plastic dinosaur he owned, launched onto the bed with an urgency not seen since we lost Woody's hat some weeks earlier. Talking of *Toy Story*, the final dinosaur he selected was a cuddly version of Rex which he picked out from his teddy-bear selection. But he couldn't take one teddy bear and leave the others, that wouldn't be fair. All the teddy bears had to go on holiday.

And so it went, on and on. Eventually, we pulled away from the house and headed for the motorway, overloaded with suit-cases containing toys and games and junk. Most of it wouldn't even be touched. Precariously balanced on the top was one carrier bag of clothes and two toothbrushes. In the boot was the Arctic survival pack that his mum packed, as you would for any expedition to the north-west of England in May.

Then came the journey itself. On the way The Boy wanted to play 'Scooby-Doo', as he did on every car journey for the next seven years. Seven long years.

These were his instructions for how to play 'Scooby-Doo' in the car:

'Right, you're Freddy as you're driving. I'll be Shaggy because I'm a boy. [Points at passing car] Look, Freddy! MONSTERS! Run! Let's play again. Right, you're Freddy as you're driving. I'll be Shaggy because I'm a boy. [Points at passing car] Look, Freddy! MONSTERS! Run! Again. Right, you're Freddy as you're driving...'

That was it. The clever part was that we repeated this, over and over, for the entire 225 miles. Four hours, no deviation, no adding in different characters, no trying to pretend that Velma has a driving licence. Just that. For the first time in my life, I missed Scrappy-Doo.

Finally, we arrived. The Boy liked Nana's house. It was a bungalow so had no horrible stairs where dark shadows might lurk at the top. Fifteen minutes after our arrival, the contents of the car were unloaded into his bedroom. The duvet cover was replaced with his own from home and the bed was moved up against the wall just like at home. And when everything was unpacked and put in its place, it could almost – almost – *be* home. Perfect.

It was difficult for both sets of grandparents in those early days, I think. Although my dad was no longer around, step-Granddad had been around since long before The Boy was born. There was something horrible about the 'step' word though, a call-back to childhood fairy tales featuring the Wicked Step-Mother. So he was very much Granddad. And no finer Granddad could The Boy have.

There were seldom hugs from his step-grandchild in the early years. No kisses. If he went too close he got hit and that was about all he could hope for in the way of contact. It must have hurt, deeply – and not always only in the physical sense. Things have changed over the years enormously, although I'm not sure when that happened. Now The Boy is renowned for his bear hugs and affection. No kisses though. Consistently inconsistent.

The difference between him and his cousins was more marked on this trip than any earlier. As they turned from being toddlers to children, a chasm seemed to be opening up between them. When my brothers and their wives visited each other's houses they were now leaving their children alone to play. The Boy though, needed more supervision than ever. I'd watch him like a hawk, looking for signs that he might attack. How awful does that sound when you're talking about your four-year-old son? As his cousins played together, he'd play side-by-side, never quite joining in, but there on the periphery. He loved their company, there was no doubt of that, he just seemed unable to know how to play. And he was always within grabbing reach. If there was a sudden spike in noise level or if an arm got perilously close to him, he'd lunge, teeth at the ready. *Not here son, please. It's the one place we've got left.*

Invariably, someone did get bitten or smacked or both. I'd make my excuses to my family and apologize, but I could see the difficulty even they had understanding him. And in the middle of it, The Boy just looked so confused. He desperately wanted to get on with his cousins, which just meant another autism myth exploded there and then. All the information I'd discovered online forever talked of the autistic child preferring solitary play, but that wasn't the case with The Boy. He loved the interaction. He just didn't know how to do it. The solitary play came about because other children gave up on him first.

We travelled back to London more confused than ever. At home, I began to withdraw into my own thoughts and the gulf between my wife and me seemed to grow larger by the day. I finally understood what people meant when they talked about being surrounded by other people but feeling completely alone.

I wanted my dad. I wanted him to tell me that everything would be OK, that love would indeed conquer all and, like that day at the theme park all those years ago, there would be victory for the little man once again.

I tried my best to avoid the monsters, Shaggy, I really did. I had my foot flat to the floor of The Mystery Machine. Maybe there were just too many.

CHAPTER EIGHT

Step Outside

Yesterday we went to see the cousins. They're roughly the same age as The Boy and they live in a small village where everyone knows everyone. They'd arranged to meet all their friends at the local park for the afternoon. They go on their own normally, on bikes or on scooters. They wanted The Boy to go with them. And he wanted to go too.

Playgrounds have always been horrible places to visit. Turn your back for a second and someone has been bitten or hit for being so bold as to want to use the slide when The Boy has decided that the very top is the perfect place to just sit and reflect on the world for twenty-five minutes. The Boy can't climb or jump, both of which come in handy in a playground. Add to that the presence of other children that he wants to be friends with but can't work out how to do it and they tend to be places of real frustration that bring out the worst in him.

So, of course we decided to go.

I drove them the fifty metres round the corner. And when we arrived we were greeted by the five other boys we were meeting there: The Gang. They were all about ten years old, all standing in their hoodies and skinny jeans. And to me they looked like they were all about twenty-three years old.

Fashion was something that largely escaped The Boy. And me. Clothes were selected for comfort only. Not that he really 'selected' clothes – he just wanted to wear the same ones. Clothing was a necessary evil, only made almost bearable by character T-shirts and Lego *Star Wars* underpants.

And, suddenly, there he was stood in the middle of all these boys with their Justin Bieber haircuts and neckerchief things. I could still make him out by the luminous socks that he always wears, poking out between too-small jogging bottoms and black school shoes that he insisted on wearing because it wasn't Saturday or Sunday. And I realized he was taller than most of them. My boy was growing up.

So, I left them to it. I sat in the car and watched from a distance, one hand on the door handle, poised. My nod towards independence. And The Boy played with them for over an hour. They seemed to laugh at his jokes that made no sense. They played tag and one of the other boys would help out when The Boy was 'it' and do the running and climbing for him. They pushed him on the swing, far higher than he'd ever let me push him and he squealed with laughter. No one was bitten. No one was hit. I'm sure he called someone a dickhead at least once, but the car windows were up, I couldn't hear and let's not spoil the romantic image. Somewhere, in a village in the middle of nowhere, for an all too brief moment in time, my son belonged.

MY SON'S NOT RAINMAN BLOG

Every Sunday morning since The Boy was born we'd gone to the park, just the two of us. It became our lads' trip out. That was the way it worked, even when me and his mum were still together – Dad would get the lie-in on a Saturday, Mum on a Sunday (except that Mum invariably had to get up on the Sunday because Dad couldn't work the pushchair or she'd want to do an emergency inspection to ensure the full change of clothes, spare nappies, bottles, first-aid kit, emergency beacon and clamps were all going along too).

I miss our trips to the park now. They were our time, the two of us. I craved the routine and comfort of every Sunday as much as The Boy did. Each week it began exactly the same way: we'd park the car at the same spot and head through the same entrance into the same park. Now, I want you to get the image right. You shouldn't imagine great avenues of tall, majestic trees and beautiful ornate benches where J. M. Barrie might have sat to first write Peter Pan. Instead, I want you to picture a backdrop of fried chicken boxes ripped apart by foxes, smatterings of different shades of dog shit and the same guy cycling round and round, dropping off small-time drug deals to anyone who wanted them. It might not be everyone's idea of a beautiful park, but it was ours.

There were rules to be followed on those Sunday mornings. Upon entering, the first thing to do was to take a sharp right turn and head to the small bridge over the stream. I say stream – it could have been a sewage outlet for all I knew. We had to stop along the way to collect twigs. The first game of the park was Poohsticks. Even when he was too little to throw his stick in the water himself we'd play Poohsticks. Mainly because I didn't know what else to do at the park. And because his mum had made it plain that she didn't want us home for two hours.

For the uninitiated, in Poohsticks you throw sticks off a bridge into the water and then dash to the other side of the bridge to see whose appears first. In those early days I used to hold The Boy over the edge of the bridge to throw his twig, legs dangling precariously over the water below. Then we'd peer over the other side to see whose twig was victorious.

'Again', he'd say, even before the twigs had reappeared. 'Again.' If ever there was a word to define what made him happy it was that one: 'Again.' Let's keep doing everything again and again and again. And again.

After we'd exhausted all the options for Poohsticks, we'd wander away from the stream and head over towards the man-made lake in the middle of the park to feed the ducks.

And it was there, on those Sunday morning outings feeding the ducks, that I suppose I first really knew you were different. There were always other children around at this point, often of a similar age to you. Much as I did with your cousins, I tried not to compare what they were doing to what you did, but I couldn't help it. I'd watch them and it was like they instinctively knew what to do with the bread. 'Little pieces,' would be the only words whispered from their parent. The children would squeal with delight, following the order. Little pieces. Tearing off small bits of bread and casting them into the water as the ducks scrambled for their food.

The Boy just used to eat the bread I'd given him. We soon learnt that we couldn't take stale, mouldy bread to feed the ducks. It had to be fresh. I remember those days of kneeling beside him, copying the other parents who all seemed to have far more of a clue what to do than I did. I muttered the words, 'Little pieces', as if he'd suddenly understand what I meant. The Boy would just look at me bemused, taking a bite out of the extra bit of breakfast. And, looking back now, it does seem strange that I expected him to grasp that when I handed him a piece of bread at home it was to eat, but when we were outside he was expected to turn it into breadcrumbs and scatter it across open water. Every now and then though I would think he'd grasped what I meant. But then he'd proceed to launch three or four whole slices of bread into the water. Along with the bag they came in.

There was, however, a species of bird The Boy liked feeding much more than the ducks. Pigeons. They were far more entertaining. As all the other children were led away from them and discouraged from giving them any food ('Dirty,' the parents would say). The Boy would plough into the middle of them, giggling and screaming. He liked pigeons – still does. Loves chasing them, desperate to catch one, is happy feeding them and strangely knows instinctively to break the bread into little pieces. It might be their flapping he likes. He used to lull them into a false sense of security, giving them pieces of bread until all their friends came over for a bit of food and then, when he was surrounded by every pigeon within a three-mile radius, he'd suddenly wave his hands and shout and the birds would all take off, flapping noisily as they went, leaving a grinning boy with a mouthful of bread laughing away in the middle.

It was a left turn after the ducks, moving along to The Wall. This was little more than a kerb really, only about two bricks high. The Boy had once watched another boy climb on to it and decided he wanted to do the same. He could never quite do it, never found his balance, never had the muscle tone. Each time Dad would bounce him along it, dangling him along the wall's edge. Next week he'll manage it. Next week…

We would move on to the café. Once he was old enough, it would be a fairy cake and orange juice for The Boy, coffee for Dad. We never sat inside. Whatever the weather, come rain or shine, you'd find the two of us in the same seats outside. A pigeon or two would join us, The Boy breaking off a bit of his cake to share with them each time. And as soon as the fairy cake was gone, so were we. No waiting around for Dad to finish his coffee. There were things to be done – not least to pay a visit to the machine with the bouncy balls.

In the entrance of the café was one of those old-style machines you often saw at the British seaside that used to contain gobstoppers. Now you often get them in posh pubs where you can buy seven M&Ms for the bargain price of 20p. Well, this one had luminous bouncy balls inside. And each week we'd buy one and each week as he gave it the first bounce it was like he was discovering the joy of a ball for the first time. The Boy would bounce his ball up and down, giggling away as he gave chase. Every now and then another child would try to join in his game, reaching down to pick up the ball or running after it to try to catch it. They were treated with absolute contempt. No matter how many times I encouraged him, there was no sharing of the bouncy ball game. It was his ball.

The park was arranged in a circle and so by this time we'd be bouncing the ball back in the general direction of the car. For a boy who so often craved predictability in life, it was the unpredictable nature of that bouncing rubber ball that used to give him the most pleasure – twisting and turning, never quite knowing where it was going to land and which direction it would spring off in next. And then suddenly, almost as quickly as it came into our life, the ball was abandoned, left on the pathway for someone else to pick up and take home. All that interest in it had suddenly gone, it had fulfilled its purpose. There were bigger fish to fry. Because, at the peak of our Sunday park adventure, we'd finally arrived… The Boy would start to point and rush forward the minute it came into view, towering over us as we neared the exit. There it was. The Magic Tree.

At first glance and to the untrained eye, The Magic Tree looked like any other tree in the park. But a select few knew its powers. For a start, you had to go right up to it, as close as you can be. And if you went right up, clasped both hands around its trunk and then wiggled yourself a little dance, The Magic Tree would start to work.

'It's not working,' The Boy would shout despondently over his shoulder, his hands wrapped tightly around the tree, bum wiggling away.

'You're not wiggling enough,' Dad would shout back, desperately rummaging through his pockets. And then it would start. Just as The Boy was giving up hope, a rustling noise would come from the branches up above his head. 'It's coming,' Dad would encourage, just as it always did. Much to The Boy's delight, money would start tumbling from The Magic Tree. If Dad had planned it right, it would be two-pence coins. Every now and then he'd curse as he had to use a ten-pence piece.

'Again, again...' The Boy would squeal with delight, running round collecting up the fortune.

'You need to wiggle some more!' Dad would shout back, moving position as The Boy retook his place around the trunk. Every now and then, if Dad was really prepared in advance, The Magic Tree would even drop individually wrapped sweets too.

I'm not sure what anyone else made of us in the park on those mornings. Walking past, seeing the small boy wiggling against the trunk of a tree while his dad stood behind him throwing money up into the branches above his head. But I started to care less and less what people thought. I knew we were different. I might have painted a rose-tinted picture of it all here, but that's because they're the memories that I want to cling to; they're the memories that for so long I'd forgotten.

Anyone walking past us on those Sunday mornings wouldn't have seen Poohsticks or magic trees. They'd have seen a young toddler screaming incessantly as each activity came to an end and his dad desperately trying to create something else to entertain him. They'd have seen the rude, badly behaved boy at the café going and sitting at the same table, even if someone was already sitting there, because that was his table and that was where they always sat. And when Dad tried to lift him away they'd have seen him hit out and scream and then sink his teeth into his dad's arm as hard as he could because for one brief moment it made things feel better on the inside.

The Magic Tree itself only came into existence because for two weeks running the machine had given us a green ball, which meant it should always be a green ball going forward, but the next time it was orange and it shouldn't have been orange, it should have been green forever. And that's what our trips out were like for so, so long. There was never enough bread, enough Poohsticks, enough 'again'. There was always too much noise and light. It was never right, no matter how hard I tried to make it so.

Despite all that, we still go the park, now and then. It's good to head back there; for too long I only remembered the bad bits.

It took The Boy's memory to remind me of the golden, joyful bits in between. Nowadays we push the wheelchair around because cerebral palsy has weakened his legs as his body has grown, meaning it's too far to walk all the way. We still follow the same route of course. The Boy will jump out of his chair for a game of Poohsticks, only disappointed at how small the bridge seems. Winning is more important than ever these days. Then he'll get back in as we head towards the ducks. In keeping with the new signage there's no bread to feed them this time – it would appear even ducks are gluten-free nowadays. He's still got no interest in them, but will charge his wheelchair at the pigeons for them to flap around him once more. Still grinning, still desperate to catch one. Then past The Wall that manages to dwarf him even in the wheelchair. He doesn't ask to climb on it now; he's learnt over the years he could never get his balance. 'Remember our wall?' he'll say as we go past it, with all the wisdom of an ageing war veteran. Memories…

Then on to the café where he's moved on to carrot cake as 'it's healthy'. He'll nod towards his old seat, 'Remember when we used to sit there?' If the seat is empty he'll take his rightful place, but he'll also sit elsewhere too. Sitting somewhere else… it's not as painful as it used to be. I can still see his discomfort but he's getting there. He still won't wait for me to finish my coffee though. As we head off, we pass the area where the bouncy ball machine used to be, since removed to make way for the redesigned buggy park and panini press. 'Remember when…?' And then, as we head back towards the car, stopping only to stroke any dog that isn't on its lead (we don't stroke dogs on leads as they have people attached to them), The Magic Tree looms into view.

The Boy kind of knows the tree isn't real anymore. About two years ago he suddenly turned round and caught me flicking a two-pence piece into the air. But I can tell by the way he looks up at its branches that he's still not really sure. And although I know he needs to grow up to be his own person, there's a part of me that wants him to believe forever. For both of us, that old tree near the exit and those Sunday morning trips to the park will always contain a little bit of magic. *Little pieces, son. Little pieces.*

CHAPTER NINE

Falling

Those with autistic traits can sometimes be mocked for their desire for routine, for consistency, for 'sameness'. But at this festive time of year I'm reminded that we all have those exact same desires for nothing to change. But if we dress it up as 'tradition' rather than 'obsession' then it becomes far more socially acceptable. 'We always have dinner at 2.00 p.m.'; 'We always open our presents first thing'; 'We always eat turkey.' Are they really any different?

I remember Christmas as a child and that feeling of wanting everything to be the same forever. Waking on a Christmas Day morning, my dad would line me and my three brothers on the stairs, oldest first. I was second in line – never before have the five minutes I arrived in this world before my twin brother been so important. Dad would get us to wait in position while he went ahead into the lounge to see if Father Christmas had been. The excitement and the tension were palpable. The 365 days since we were last stood in this spot had all just been building suspense for this moment to come around again. Dad would open the lounge door, just enough for him to step inside but not enough for us to see no matter how hard we strained our necks over the bannister. I'm sure the silence that followed only lasted seconds, but at the time it felt like forever.

'Oh, no. No. Please, no.' He'd step back into the hall, disappointment etched on his face. 'Mum!' he'd call up the stairs, 'You need to come down. I'm sorry, boys. He hasn't been. I don't know what we're going to do. There's nothing for you. I'm so sorry, lads. You'd better come and see.'

Every Christmas of my childhood this ritual was performed. Yet every year we believed him. And then we'd file into the lounge and by the light of the Christmas tree we'd discover that he had very much been after all. 'Happy Christmas, boys,' Dad would say, his grinning face lighting the dark corners of the room that the tree lights didn't reach.

During my lifetime I've now had more Christmases without Dad around than I spent with him. And he probably never realized it at the time, but those few moments of routine on Christmas Day morning have left an indelible mark. Dad constantly worried that he wasn't educated enough, didn't earn enough or wasn't good enough. As parents we spend so much time worrying about the big things that sometimes we forget the small ones. I don't even remember the presents

I received each year. But if anyone ever asks me to define the true meaning of happiness in my life, it will forever be shaped by the memory of standing on the stairs on a cold December morning, waiting to see if *he's* been.

MY SON'S NOT RAINMAN BLOG

I 'll warn you in advance, the contents of this chapter might come as a bit of a shock, or seem as though they've come from nowhere. Or maybe not. Maybe the events that I'm about to describe will come as no surprise. I just know that I can't tell our story without this bit – I'd be self-editing a story that I really want to come from a place of truth. Be gentle with me, dear reader.

It's fair to say that those early years took their toll on me and on The Boy's mum, too, I'm sure. And I honestly don't know how she did it. The truth is, I found being a dad incredibly hard. I think everyone had always assumed I'd be so good at it – I was, I suppose, a natural kids' entertainer, probably because I spent most of my adult life wishing I was still a child myself. But it turns out there's more to parenting than blowing raspberries and playing peek-a-boo.

My moods had been legendary over the years, particularly when I was a child. I always thought I was just a bit emotionally immature; I couldn't quite express myself the way other people could. I cried too often if I thought someone was upset or angry with me and, if I'm honest, I still do. I thought I was just over-sensitive. I cried when John Noakes, my favourite television presenter, left *Blue Peter*, my favourite television programme; I cried when Mr Scott wasn't our head teacher anymore and I cried when some unsuspecting homeowner returned home to discover they'd had a garden makeover by a television crew. To be fair, it was always the water feature that did it – I used to imagine how my dad would react if he got his very own fountain with a bronze heron and underwater lighting. And when I look back now, I realize I never wanted to cry as much as I did in those early years after The Boy was born. For whatever reason, my mood was slipping and I didn't want to face up to it.

I've tried to analyse what happened, work out what the cause was, but I'm still not sure. Sometimes, the more I think about it, the more I throw up questions that I can't hope to answer. I remember years ago, as a child, watching a film with my dad on a Saturday afternoon. Actually, scrap that, it must have been a Sunday – Saturday was his treat day, watching horse racing on the television and having his favourite lunch of pork chops, chips and peas with HP Sauce over the lot. I thought he was so clever because he could shake the bottle of sauce and spread its dark brown goodness over his food without getting big splodges in the wrong places. I was still a large-dollop-of-red-ketch-up-in-the-corner-of-the-plate kind of kid and I watched him those Saturday afternoons, vowing that one day I would be old enough to have my dinner on a tray and, when I did, I would learn to like white pepper and I would do that trick with the HP Sauce too.

Yes, thinking back to it, it was definitely a Sunday, before the tea trolley came out with sandwiches and a cheesy family game show came on the telly. There was a film about elephants and, although I suppose it must have been fiction, it felt incredibly real and I've always wanted it to remain that way. It was about how the elephants, when their lives come to an end, go behind a waterfall to die. As they feel the moment approaching, they up and leave their family and begin the long, slow pilgrimage to the Other Side. When they finally reach the waterfall, they pass through it to the dark, mysterious cave behind, lay their exhausted bodies down and drift off to an endless sleep.

Somewhere, behind the waterfalls of this world, if you search hard enough, would be huge caves filled with the bones and ivory of those elephants that have passed on. For the child who broke his heart at the television makeover crew turning over a flower bed, you can imagine what that film did to me that day. I was broken. I did what I always did when we watched TV as a family: I lay on the floor in front of the gas fire with my head in my hands, facing the television so that no one could see my face and I made sure my shoulders didn't shake as that would have given the game away. Much as I did when John Noakes announced he was going, I silently wept my heart out.

Ever since that day, elephants have embodied a sadness for me. It's there in their eyes, the way they seem to carry the weight of the world on their shoulders, like they know from the moment they're born that each step is simply taking them closer to the cave behind the waterfall. I'm banging on a bit here to make my point, but I guess it's this: when The Boy was born, there was a part of me that felt it was my time to lie down behind the waterfall. My work and purpose on this planet was done – I had procreated, I had made my contribution to the circle of life and now it was time to pass the baton on. Something like that anyway. It seems almost daft admitting it now I've written it down.

Maybe I'm reading too much into things again. Maybe The Boy being born simply reminded me of my own dad and brought my own childhood into focus and that chasm between those living and those who have passed on. Or maybe I was just a lazy sod who didn't want to face up to a life of responsibility and organic pureed food. I'm not sure.

Whatever the reason, I knew my mood was slipping. I was retreating into myself more and more. I suppose I just felt so… inadequate. We were struggling financially and my wife had to return to work. I felt responsible, like I wasn't man enough. Maybe if I earned a bit more I'd feel less useless around the house. The Boy invariably wanted his mum – she appeared to have the patience of a saint whereas I couldn't settle him, couldn't quieten his darker moments. Maybe because when I held him in my arms, he could sense the unease that seemed to be pouring out of my body.

I stopped going to work. I can't remember how it happened and how much of a conscious decision it was; I just didn't get up one morning. I didn't call them – I just didn't go in. It wasn't out of rudeness, I'd got myself into what I thought at the time was a state of self-pity where I didn't think anyone would really notice if I was there or not. I'd just have a bit of a lie-in and go in later. Or maybe tomorrow. Or Wednesday...

I stayed in bed for days. Eventually, the days turned into weeks. And, although I know we are constantly told we shouldn't be ashamed of mental illness, there's a huge part of me that is, even as I write this now. I didn't want to include this in this book. I told myself it wasn't relevant, it wasn't part of our story. But if I'm honest it's because there's still a very real part of me that doesn't want to own what happened. Even now, years later, admitting that I lay in bed for weeks on end shames me more than I can tell you. My poor ex-wife... no one will ever really know the impact of that time on her. For all our differences, she will forever have all my love and gratitude for everything she did.

And you, son, what was the effect on you? The million dollar question, the one that I ask myself each and every day. There are darker times when I've wondered if everything that has followed since that day has somehow been my fault, that it's all been caused by the man who one day decided to hide under his duvet and forget the world for a while. I've learnt to be a bit more forgiving of myself with time. My overriding hope looking back is that the effect on you was minimal, that the overwhelming strength of your mum's love meant you barely noticed.

As I spent all my time in bed, I began to lose my grip on reality. My body refused to sleep constantly, so instead I ended up lying there, as days and nights tumbled into one and I started to ruminate, thinking things over and over, creating my own form of reality from the little bits of the world that once in a while invaded my space. I heard the phone ring downstairs and the concerned calls from work soon turned into people laughing at me.

The paranoia is what I remember the most, the unmistakable knowledge that everyone was out to get me, to expose me as a fraud to the world. And all the time I thought I could stop it at any point; I kept thinking I'd get up in a minute and that would be the end of it. I'd have a shower, go downstairs, take The Boy for a walk and then head into work and everything would be fine. I wasn't ill; I'd just got off the ride for a while. I'd get back on in a minute, I'd just stay here for a while.

Eventually the GP came round. And then the community mental health team. What could I say to them? I couldn't tell them I was an elephant on my way to the cave behind the waterfall. I didn't know how to put any of it into words. And if I tried to speak I thought I'd cry and cry and the tears would never stop. So, the longer I became trapped in my own reality, the safer it became. I refused their antidepressants, refused to answer the door when they called round in the daytime and my wife was at work and The Boy at nursery. I ventured downstairs each day to turn the volume down on the phone and take the batteries out of the doorbell. Then I'd retreat back under the duvet and if I lay perfectly still I could convince myself I didn't exist at all.

It wasn't long before I lost every last sense of what was real and what wasn't. I'm not even sure how long I was in that bedroom before things finally came to a head. The paranoia was taking over, I remember that much. It was early summer, the odd fly would come into the room and I became convinced that they were spies fitted with miniature cameras, sent by either my employer or the medical community. Neither could be trusted. Everyone became the enemy. The conversations I had been having with myself in my head for weeks on end finally spilled out and I began talking to myself out loud. I'd lost it.

I remember one morning in particular. There was a hive of activity in the house, I could hear voices downstairs, all talking away. And I remember not being sure if they were real or not and how frightening that felt. By this point I knew I'd become unwell, but it still felt like something I'd created. I thought I could snap myself out of it. If I'd just got up and gone to work that day, none of this would have happened.

Eventually the voices came into the room. A consultant psychiatrist, a psychiatric nurse, my GP and a social worker. What a party. And as they walked in, a fly followed them through the door. A sign, if I needed one, that they were bad people.

I hid under the duvet, buried myself from them and, as they talked, I tried to escape further and further into my own world. The psychiatric nurse, a sweet gentle Irish man who shared my name and who, even then, I felt was one of the good people, reached down and I felt his hand on my back through the duvet. 'You're not well, John. We think some time in hospital might help you.' Like the old days watching television in front of the gas fire, I made sure he didn't know it, but there was something about his manner that reached me that day. In the darkness I kept my shoulders still and the tears poured down my face. 'OK,' I mumbled from under the duvet, 'I'll go this afternoon.'

I sensed they didn't believe me. After all, it wasn't the first time they'd suggested hospital admission; the community mental health team had tried to persuade me some weeks earlier. 'We'd like you to go now, John,' the consultant psychiatrist said. He tried to do the soft, gentle voice that came so naturally to John the nurse, but he hadn't quite mastered it. To my ears there was an edge of menace in his manner. 'There's an ambulance outside to take you.'

Eventually, I agreed. I kept trying to delay things – something about the psychiatrist had put me on edge and heightened the paranoia. 'I'll just have a cigarette' and 'I'll just get changed.'

They told me the ambulance was waiting, so after some persuasion I gave in and for the first time in weeks, even months, I stepped outside the front door of the house. The world seemed somewhat different that day; not quite real. I can't describe it.

The one unmistakably real thing though was the ambulance, parked in front of the gate. It looked out of place, like they always do when they're in familiar surroundings. It was like a scene from *Doctor Who* when you see the Tardis in the middle of modern-day Cardiff. Behind it, parked slightly up the road, was a police car, but I thought nothing of that. This was southeast London after all.

As I stepped into the ambulance I went to sit down on one of the drop-down seats near the rear doors. 'You'll have to lie on the bed, I'm afraid,' said the medic. 'There aren't enough seats.'

I shrugged and got onto the stretcher.

He immediately pulled some large red straps across me, tying me down so my arms and legs couldn't move. 'Go easy, mate,' I said, 'I'm not bloody Hannibal Lecter!' No one laughed.

I noticed my wife sitting opposite. It was the first time I'd really looked at her in weeks. She smiled at me, but it was just her mouth moving. Her eyes didn't change. She looked so tired, so sad. The social worker stepped into the ambulance, taking up a seat near the rear doors. As soon as she stepped in, the technician pulled the doors shut, gave the all-clear to the driver and we started to pull away. I noticed the police car following through the rear window. The social worker cleared her throat with a little cough, then began a speech that she'd no doubt delivered many times before:

'John, I am informing you that you are being detained under section two of the Mental Health Act...'

I'm sure there was more to her speech, but her voice seemed to trail off into the background as my wife reached out and held my hand. She gave it a little squeeze. I don't know if it was the reality of it or if it was that first human contact in weeks, but I turned away to face the side of the ambulance. I tried my hardest to not let anyone see but my shoulders shook uncontrollably up and down and, for the first time in my life, it felt like they might never stop.

CHAPTER TEN

The Long Climb

Sometimes, it takes time away to appreciate all that you have. We had another brilliant holiday up north with family. We visited the same old places we always visit, but this trip was different. I'm not sure what it was but, after everything that's happened, those few days away made the world seem OK again. After months of reading and writing reports and assessments that endlessly detail all that The Boy can't do, I'd forgotten to keep looking for everything he can. And it made me realize that if you spend your life focusing on everything that's wrong, you might just miss everything that's right.

While we were away we revisited an aquarium we'd been to when The Boy was younger. He didn't remember having been there before, but I did. He was around six and, having spent £20 to get in, we spent a total of twelve seconds in there, with him shouting one long 'NEMO!' at the top of his voice as he ran the length of the place before we exited out to the daylight at the other end. This time, the darkness didn't bother him so much and we stopped to look at each tank, taking everything in – we even sat through the sea-lion show. I hadn't noticed it before, but there's an inquisitiveness to him nowadays, a desire for knowledge that was always missing as a toddler. And as I looked around at the enthralled three-year-olds sitting around us watching the sea lion jump for the ball, I realized our lives weren't so different. I can't quite explain it, but in some ways it just feels like we're living our lives on a different time trajectory to everyone else, that's all. Like The Boy will get there eventually – he's just following a different path.

There was so much we did in those few days. We caught up with family we hadn't seen for a long time. Their reaction to seeing The Boy is always the same – they're always struck by how much he's grown, but also by his similarity to me. Despite how often I'm told it, I can never see it myself, but apparently we don't just share the same dashing good looks, but the same mannerisms, even the same sense of humour. Nowadays The Boy's mum often refers to him as Mini-John. How blessed he is.

We went to a barbecue where The Boy had his first go in a hot tub and then refused to get out until his skin had turned blue. And, back at Nana's house, The Boy played endlessly with Monty the dog, lying on him, pulling him, and apparently teaching him to ballroom dance.

Magical times.

But the highlight of our holidays were our trips to the sea-side together. Short day trips away – the seaside was only twenty minutes from Nana's house. And those days with The Boy reminded me of my own childhood more than ever.

We went on an open-top bus tour and had the whole top deck to ourselves, trying to scream as loud as we could into the wind....

A seagull nicked the Boy's chips on the seafront as we sat and watched a Punch and Judy Show, then I wheeled The Boy along the pier in his wheelchair, racing unsuspecting old people in their mobility scooters. We found an old joke shop Dad used to visit as a little boy, and we bought some fake poo and a fart whistle. Neither of us knew what a fart whistle was until that day, but it's become such a part of our lives since that it now seems strange to imagine a world without it.

But the highlight of it all was when we returned a few days later. When we go to the seaside we usually park outside the George Hotel – named, apparently, in honour of The Boy's cousin. Well, this day there were no spaces, so we found ourselves in an unfamiliar part of town. As we were walking along to the seafront, I spotted something – a fish and chip café I remembered going to as a child that I thought had long gone. Thirty years later, there it was, on the corner, where it had stood all this time.

The Boy didn't need any convincing to go inside. His esca-pade with the seagull a couple of days earlier had put him off al fresco dining for life. We took a table in the corner, exactly where we'd sat as a family, a generation ago.

And it was there, in that café, that I finally saw what everyone else has been telling me since The Boy was born. As he tucked into his fish and chips he looked up at me and grinned. How had I missed it for so long? It was plain as day. Sitting opposite me was me as a child, exactly the same age. Unmistakable. Smiling away, looking up into my dad's eyes and knowing there was no place on Earth I'd rather be.

And as I sit here writing this now, I can hear my dad's voice once more, bringing me back down to earth with a bump. 'How much? Eighteen quid for two portions of fish and chips!? Christ on a bike, son, you'll never be me.'

MY SON'S NOT RAINMAN BLOG

Daylight. Sleeping. Screaming. Olanzapine. Tests. Hospitals. Line up. Therapy. Making good progress. Scared. Laughing. Government agents. Lamotrigine. Day release. Voices. Fear. Smiles. Kindness. Canteens. Medication trolleys. Lithium. Surreal. Doctors. Brain scans. Paranoia. Nightmares. Despair. Venlafaxine. Spies. Tremors. Relapse. Home treatment teams. Dry mouth. Fifteen-minute observations. Psychosis. Risperidone. The black mouse. Reality. My Boy. My beautiful boy.

Over the next two years I was in and out of three different hospitals. I heard voices, I saw things that weren't real, I had moments where I was the Lord of all creation and then returned to the absolute nothing of nothingness. I spent my time on locked wards, under twenty-four-hour observation and, finally, thanks to an incredibly generous and understanding employer, sitting side-by-side with D-list celebrities in therapy sessions in a private psychiatric hospital.

I was given numerous diagnoses from different experts in those two years. Psychotic depression, schizophrenia, schizo-affective disorder. In the end, they settled on bipolar disorder. I didn't really care what label they put on it – it didn't change the lithium or huge doses of antipsychotics I was put on. Turns out, if you're a big bloke, it can take a fair old dose to reach the desired effect. I resented taking their medications and maybe recovery would have come quicker if I hadn't. But I could never quite explain it to medical professionals, this need to see how I felt without mind-altering medications. I was forever trying to stop taking them, simply because I needed to know if I could get back to me. I mean, the real 'me', the 'me' I was before it all started. For quite some time, I couldn't.

Sadly there's no 'cut', 'copy' and 'paste' in life, no matter how much we might wish there was sometimes. For so long all I ever wanted was a window to pop up to ask, 'Are you sure you want to delete 2005–7 and all its contents?' And never has that been truer than when sitting here in front of Microsoft Word, knowing that with a few clicks I could just erase this chapter and the chapter before it. But happen they did and the ramifications of those events continue to this day.

There are so many memories of that period flying round in my head – all disjointed, all muddled up. I remember being in one hospital endlessly laughing with other patients as we sat around one evening watching *One Flew Over the Cuckoo's Nest* in the TV room, casting each other in the different roles, the irony of our surroundings making it all the funnier. I remember the kindness of nurses who sat with me at 4.00 a.m. while thoughts swirled around my head, never quite making the journey into words. And I remember the air ambulance landing one afternoon, sadly too late for the fellow patient who found their own exit route in the bathroom with a razor blade.

I mentioned earlier that I don't know the impact of that time on The Boy. He was around three years of age when it all began, too young to remember most of it, I think (and secretly hope). Every weekend he came to visit me in different hospitals, never on the ward, if I'm honest because I didn't want him seeing the other patients. They were mad – not like me. Invariably we sat next to fish tanks in waiting rooms or, as I got better, in the garden or we went to the park. I looked forward to Saturdays more than anything. Without fail, he'd arrive with his mum. His smile, picking him up, me burying my nose in his neck, the smell of him bringing me closer to reality than any antipsychotic or therapy session ever could. He smelt of home.

I've probably said enough. This book, this story – it was never really meant to be about me. I don't want to whitewash what happened, but I don't want it to take over everything either.

For now, it feels right to leave it there. My recovery from those days of mental illness has been a parallel story, not necessarily a different one. I should state that at the time of writing this, I'm well and have been for quite some time. I haven't taken any medication for around seven years and I've not seen a psychiatrist in over four years. There was no miracle cure – I'm still far too sensitive, prone to mood swings and rubbish at relationships. And, although it pains the working-class man in me to say it, a long time in therapy helped.

It took a while to get used to the process. Sitting there, banging on about myself for fifty minutes. I never told anybody for years where I was vanishing to – sneaking away to spend my time in tiny consulting rooms that always looked identical; two IKEA chairs, a sign about confidentiality and a strategically placed box of tissues. Slowly, over time, with a psychotherapist I learnt to both love and hate in equal measure, I began to make sense of stuff. And maybe that's the word to best describe what happened. Stuff (I'm sure there's a more eloquent way to put it, but please bear in mind I originally wanted to write 'shit', so let's look on the word 'stuff' as an improvement).

No matter how much I tell myself that what happened wasn't my fault, every now and again I still feel a pang of guilt from that period, although not so much nowadays. Such is the stigma of mental illness, I suppose. With or without his autism, I will always wonder about the impact that my strange behaviour may have had on The Boy during such an important developmental stage.

As children we often look up to our parents and think they're going to live forever. We place our hand in theirs and know the world will be OK. It's only years later that we get a sense of their own fallibility, their own weaknesses. Other people are so often right – there is so much that binds me and The Boy; the shared sense of humour, the impulsiveness, even the same little birthmark we both have. But maybe the biggest thing we share is often overlooked by everyone. It's our vulnerability.

CHAPTER ELEVEN

Separate Lives

I'm appalling at DIY. Appalling. If ever anything breaks in this house, the best The Boy can hope for is that his dad will write a very nice letter of complaint to someone. I don't own a toolkit. Somewhere in one of the kitchen cupboards there is a hammer. In the dark recesses of the airing cupboard there might still be a spanner. The screwdriver hasn't been seen since it was used to change a battery at Christmas.

Last year we ordered a new sofa. It arrived, and then I realized I had to get rid of the old sofa. I was going to free-cycle it, but after endless Power Ranger battle re-enactments, it was no longer fit for human use. It was time to send it to the sofa graveyard.

The local council wanted £15 and two days' notice to remove it. Fifteen quid! Two days' notice! Looking back now, it seems a reasonable amount. At the time, though, I thought it was a rip-off. I'm not paying that. I would get rid of it for less. I was a man. With a car. It couldn't be that hard to chop up a sofa small enough to fit into a Toyota Aygo. I would chop it up and take it to the tip myself. Like a real man would.

To keep costs down, I decided to do it all in one car journey. I began by smuggling out the cushions and backs with the other rubbish. I had to do it carefully, so as not to raise suspicion from the bin men. As in *The Great Escape* when the heroes tip the rubble from digging tunnels out of their pockets as they walk, I hid a cushion in each bin bag as I left them out. After just seven weeks, I was left with only the sofa frame standing upright in the lounge. What a winner.

I could still have paid the £15 but that was, of course, for losers. All I needed was something to chop up the frame. I went to the supermarket, where all the top men go for their DIY supplies and bought a handsaw for £5.99. I came home and started hacking at the frame. I was shocked to discover that it had foam inside it. I never knew. And it turned out you couldn't cut foam with a handsaw. Or nail scissors. I nipped back out to the shops and picked up a pair of big scissors (I think that's the technical term for them) for £3.99. Oh, and I needed some strong bin bags, of course, to put the bits of sofa in. I'd need the really strong ones – £4.29. I think I must have ended up putting the big scissors in one of the bin bags too, because they haven't been seen since.

I continued hacking away. Sofas are stronger than you might think. After another couple of weeks of work, I managed to saw it in half, so it now took up double the space in the lounge and the handsaw was knackered. That's OK, I thought, I'll buy a jigsaw. I reasoned that it would come in handy in the future if I ever needed to chop some furniture in half again. I went back to the supermarket – £17.99. That'll show the council and their extortionate fifteen quid. It cut the wood brilliantly.

I made another shocking discovery a couple of weeks later. Sofas have things inside them called 'springs' and springs are made of metal. My jigsaw wouldn't cut through metal. And I know, because I tried. After another few weeks of research, I went to the local hardware store to buy some metal cutters. They cost me £19.99, but that didn't matter, because by now I was a man possessed. I would show the world that I was a real man. A real man capable of chopping his own sofa into pieces if he chose to.

Today, it is nine months since the new sofa was delivered. And, as I write, the last remaining bin bag of the old sofa sits next to me, ready to be removed. In just 273 days and at a total cost of £56.54 (I needed more bin bags), I have won the battle. I have successfully stuck two fingers up to the council and their rip-off fifteen quid charge.

I'm only telling you this story because sometimes The Boy will act in a certain way and people will say, 'Oh, it's because he's autistic.' Well, it isn't. Not always. There will be periods in his life when The Boy will do some really, really stupid things. And sometimes it will be nothing to do with his autism. Sometimes, it's just genetics.

My wife and I separated in the summer, not long after The Boy's fourth birthday, a few months after my final stay in hospital. It feels like I should state, 'There were no other people involved,' as that's what's said at moments like this. But there was very much someone else involved: The Boy. There was an unbearable sadness on both parts. If nothing else, sadness that we'd let him down, that we were no different from anyone else who'd said they 'couldn't meet his needs'. People have asked if it was him, if he was the cause of the marriage breakdown. No. Absolutely not. Circumstances didn't help, certainly, but it could never be him. Whatever the reasons, they were only connected to his mum and me.

It was a difficult time in lots of ways. I went to stay with my mate Greg in north London. He and his lovely wife Susie put me up for a few weeks. And it's so true what they say: you don't realize what you have until it's gone. I'd have done anything to be woken at 5.00 a.m. by the sound of the Disney Channel. I missed The Boy's cry, his laugh, his smile, his screams. I missed picking dried-in breakfast cereal off the ceilings and walls. I just missed him.

Every Saturday I'd make my way across London on the bus and train to see him. And each Saturday I'd take him out because that's what dads do on their weekend visits. Part-time parenting. We'd trundle off on a bus and then go and sit in McDonald's for seven minutes, as that's about how long he could sit in one place in those days. Then we'd get up and look at something else. We'd go to a museum up the road to look at the fish in the aquarium. Most children would wander round there for an hour but we were in and out in four minutes. Museum done. Truth was, we both hated those Saturday outings.

There are all kinds of experts who have written that those with autism have a lack of empathy, how they have no 'theory of mind' and fail to imagine a world outside themselves. Personally, I think it's a load of bollocks. If anything, it has always felt like The Boy is *too* empathetic. He's always fed off the moods around him. I'm constantly having to watch the pitch in my voice, ensuring it doesn't sound angry or sad as he will react. Those Saturday outings were miserable for both of us. And they were miserable because I was miserable. As parents, we make the weather in all this, I have no doubt about that.

That said, there was one brilliant bright spot during that time that's definitely worth talking about. It was on those long, cold Saturdays that we discovered The Boy loved a train ride. There was something reassuring about the noise they made, the movement of the carriages, the fact they never deviated and always followed the same route. Or perhaps I'm playing the autism card, as that's what I've read those with the condition like, and it was just because sitting on the train was a whole lot warmer than trudging the streets. Or maybe he just liked trains.

Lots of kids do. Living in London has its benefits now and again and one of them is that if you like a train ride, you're spoilt for choice. Granted, there's often a replacement bus service in place at the weekends, but for the most part trains shoot off in every direction all of the time. But there was one route in particular that stole his heart – the Docklands Light Railway.

Now, let me explain for the uninitiated, the Docklands Light Railway *has trains with no drivers*. That's right, a driverless train. Who wouldn't get excited by that? It's known as the DLR for short: Disney's Last Ride. I accept that there's no driver because of the technological advancements that have been made in railways. But to a four-year-old autistic boy and his immature father, there's no driver because that work of beauty standing on the platform with its red livery is a Magic Train.

That's right, son. Your dad loves you that much that he's taking you for a ride on the cheap-as-arseholes, warm, Magic Train.

There's only one seat to be had on a train with no driver, of course, and that's the front seat. As there is no cab in the DLR trains, you can sit at the front and look straight out through the large windows onto the track as if you were in the driver's seat yourself. The two of us waited on the platform in pole position and, as soon as the train doors opened, we flung pregnant women out of the way to get to the seat.

'Sorry, flower,' I paused to apologize over my shoulder as we boarded, 'this lad's got a dream.'

We jostled our way through the carriage and took our seats at the front of the train, just the windscreen between the two of us and the straight track stretching out ahead. It was time for the pièce de résistance. I opened up the small rucksack that I was carrying (I had craftily told his mum at handover it contained some drinks, change of clothes and a first-aid kit) and I pulled out a small child's plastic steering wheel that I'd picked up from Argos en route. I attached it with rubber suckers to the windscreen in front of us.

Right sunshine, here we go. You and me, kiddo, we're not just passengers on the Magic Train. We're going to drive the bloody thing! And, as that train moved along the tracks, if you believed enough, if you just believed…

It felt like it took off into the air. As if we soared higher and higher. On those Saturday afternoons we pushed the fur coats aside and rode on through the back of the wardrobe.

'Hello, Mr Tumnus!' I'd shout out, pointing into the distance. 'Hello, Aslan! Hello, magical, mystical towers… of Canary Wharf.'

We took a left turn at the Magic Faraway Tree before we climbed a little higher to Neverland.

And it was there, son, riding the DLR, where I realized how lucky I was to have you in my life. As you huddled in close, with us both in our green parkas, there were moments where I couldn't tell where I ended and you began. I don't think our future had ever felt more precarious, yet life had never felt more real or more pure.

And then he spoiled the moment. In just five words, The Boy would suddenly ruin it all. 'Can I drive now, Daddy?'

Looking back, we both needed a bit of escape on those Saturday afternoons.

Eventually, we'd ridden ourselves to the point of exhaustion and I dropped him back home again, ready to do it all again the week after.

That was the worst bit, saying 'Goodbye' on the doorstep. Batman never had to say goodbye to Robin, and even the Lone Ranger had Tonto. I'd like to pretend it was the times he cried as I left that were the hardest. But they weren't. It was the times he didn't that hurt more.

I knew I had to get my own place; we couldn't carry on like this. I scoured the area looking for somewhere local and affordable. And then I found a flat. It all happened surprisingly quickly and I moved that November. I negotiated the rent with the landlord to include a bed and a sofa and I brought some things from our former house: my books and a portable TV. I really wanted the Le Creuset griddle pan, but it just felt wrong to ask.

It was my first time living alone, ever. The Boy's mum came round to carry out the all-important health and safety inspection before he was allowed to visit. The new home had to have her seal of approval. Plug protectors were needed. And window locks. And cupboard guards. And safety strips to prevent fire doors closing on trapped fingers. I nodded along, writing them all down on a scrap of paper, knowing none of them would ever be bought. We'd just get by.

The Boy loved the flat. I was so worried he'd hate it, seeing none of his familiar things. I felt like an estate agent showing him around on his first trip, desperate for him to like it. It didn't look like a home, but the emptiness was precisely what made it home for him. No clutter, no unnecessary objects getting in the way, just freedom to run around and make noise. It was also just around the corner from his mum's house and he would be close to school – same park, same familiar shops, same, same, same. Even the fact that there was no bed in his room didn't faze him.

And there I was, thirty-five years of age, finally feeling like I was a grown-up. That first time when he came over and we closed the door to the outside world, that was it. Much like that moment when we drove home from hospital for the first time all those years earlier, here we were. A family. Until that point, it felt like I was pretending at being a parent; his mum was always around if he got too much. But this was it. It's just you and me, kid.

It wasn't perfect, the arrangement with two homes, it never would be, but it worked as well as it could. His mum and I had discussions around shared care and decided to start slowly. At first The Boy came over to my flat every other weekend and one night in the week. I think Mum was nervous as I wasn't that long out of hospital and this was all new for all of us, not least The Boy.

We spent that Christmas together, 'for The Boy's sake,' as we have every Christmas since. And birthdays. I can't pretend it's always been easy, because it hasn't. Like so much in this world, it isn't necessarily better or worse than the life I'd envisaged. It's just different.

That December I got a bonus from work, not much but enough to kit out a flat with the basics from IKEA and I borrowed items from friends. The Boy finally got his bed, which was when he came for his first overnight stay. In some ways, he was more settled than he ever had been at the house. The house was too big for him. He always preferred small and he loves Nana's bungalow, flats and caravans. His new bedroom had the lounge on one side and my bedroom on the other. He was never more than a couple of feet away from another person and that was just the way he liked it. There were fewer places for the monsters to hide. And perhaps what really swung it, from the moment he moved in, was that he could reach the light switches.

Night-time has always been the enemy for The Boy. It was not so much darkness as the shadows he didn't like. In the corners of rooms, in the recesses, that's where the monsters lurked. And when the lines between reality and make-believe are forever blurred, those monsters can seem only too real.

From the first night he stayed, a bedtime routine began that has remained in place ever since. As the light begins to fade outside, all cupboards must be closed. Tightly. Wardrobe doors shut. To keep the darkness inside them. He will close them himself nowadays, but there was a time when he couldn't even bring himself to do that for fear of something reaching out and grabbing him. We have to do a sweep of the flat together in silence, me in front, him pointing to each offending piece of furniture in turn. We finish with the bed, the final check for monsters underneath, before the all-clear. Not so long ago I wondered where his old teddies had gone from the bottom of his bed and then I found them. They were stuffed down the side of the bed next to empty Lego boxes, to fill the gap where the shadows form when no one is looking.

He also starts turning on lights, preparing for the imminent onslaught of darkness. Time to flood the place with light. Every light. Except for table lamps or bedside lamps – they're redundant in this flat, as is any form of ambient illumination. Their light is too soft, forming sinister shadows that dance across the walls and leave too many corners unlit. No, it must be the ceiling lights. Without lampshades. Bright. Clinical. And, although cupboard doors must be closed, room doors are different; they must be flung open, as open as can be to ensure there's nowhere to hide behind them.

Once night-time has arrived no room door can be closed. They must all be wide open, almost turning the flat into one giant studio. Bathroom, kitchen, bedrooms, all doors wedged open, all lit brightly. I can almost hear Grandad's voice from beyond the grave, shuddering at the thought of all that wasted electricity seeping out of every bulb. 'Do you think we're made of bloody money? Christ, it's like bloody Las Vegas in here.' But at least there's nowhere for the demons of the dark to hide.

Once The Boy's happy with the state of the flat and we've had a forty-minute fight about brushing teeth, he goes to bed. And, after going to all that trouble to ensure the flat is brighter than an operating theatre, he buries himself deep under his duvet. Then he builds a tent out of three pillows and burrows his head under there too. It's too dark for shadows under there. Finally he can sleep, safe in the knowledge that nothing can reach him because on the other side of his makeshift tent he's surrounded by light.

After half an hour of silence from the bedroom, Dad will decide the coast is clear. In the lounge he'll finally get the chance to remove his sunglasses and click the ceiling light off. The shadows from the flickering TV skitter across the walls – the light spilling in from the open kitchen door and hallway is more than enough to illuminate the room. Almost immediately, in the room next door, a monster stirs. Feet pad across the hall and, silently, a hand reaches around the door frame, flicking the switch back on.

Dad should have learnt by now, The Boy has told him often enough. Always leave the lights on and little monsters sleep.

CHAPTER TWELVE

The Doctor Will See You Now

The Boy got soaked on our way back from the shops this morning. Mainly because Crap Dad forgot his coat. As we walked home the sun came out and he dried off. Or, to put it in his words, 'All the wet has gone off me.'

He was chatty today. And inquisitive. The chatty bit happens quite often, normally about something he's seen on the Internet or a *Doctor Who* fact that suddenly needs sharing. But the inquisitive bit is a treat to be savoured, a rarity. This is the boy who'd rather spend his days at school locking himself in a toilet than acquiring knowledge. Knowledge is something to be gained in secret from a computer screen when no one is looking, not something to be learnt from a person. But today he wanted to know stuff. He wanted to know about The Past.

The Past is a big confusing mess to The Boy. Anything and everything that took place before today happened 'a long time ago'. Something that happened yesterday is now confined to the same time frame as ten years ago. And events that happened before he was born are just inconceivable to him. In The Boy's eyes the world and everything in it was created the very same day he was.

The other day we drove past his nursery. The Boy went there eight years ago. And as we drove past a child was coming out of the door. She must have been around two years of age. 'Who's she?' The Boy said. 'I don't remember her! She must be new. I hope my friends are looking after her.' So, we talked about how none of his friends are there anymore, how they've all grown up like he has and how he won't know anybody in the nursery now.

And this talk of the past has obviously been playing on his mind, because today he asked me about when I was a child. So, I told him all about how Nana is my mum and I lived with her and his uncles who are my brothers, together with The Grandad Who Isn't Here Anymore. And he wanted to know more. He asked about our house and the garden, and what the bedrooms were like. I finally got the chance to tell my son how tough it was in the olden days and how we had bunk beds and no heating, but we were 'appy.

The conversation lasted about seven minutes. Seven glorious, golden minutes. He asked more questions, about who shared a bedroom with who, and who I sat next to at the dinner table. And it seemed to be sinking in, this idea of a past without him, he finally seemed to be getting it. Then suddenly he became more animated. 'Who did I sit next to at dinner?' he asked. 'Did I have a bunk bed too?'

Ah, well, there's always tomorrow, when today will become yesterday too. *In many ways you're right, son. There was no world before you.*

MY SON'S NOT RAINMAN BLOG

I touched on it earlier, the strange emotions it stirs inside me when I'm delving into the past. Long-forgotten memories suddenly flood my every thought.

It's particularly true when it comes to The Boy's behaviour – I don't know if it's intentional or just the mind protecting itself, but I'd almost forgotten just how difficult it was. When I was dealing with so-called challenging behaviour on a daily basis it just becomes the norm.

I remember years later being at an appointment and we were asked how things were going 'behaviour-wise'. The Boy's mum replied that things had become much better and that The Boy was hitting out far less. The doctor then pointed out that he'd hit his mum seven times during the ten minutes we'd been in the room. It wasn't that we were glossing over it or trying to deceive the doctor. I suppose it was just that we had become so accustomed to it that we tended not to notice if it wasn't a major event. I guess it's a bit like living with a chronic condition – there's an underlying pain each day that you become adjusted to, so it becomes the norm. It's only the spikes in pain that are recorded.

I always said the whole idea of telling our story was to make sure these behaviours didn't define him and going back over them is proving a challenge in itself. And today it's wound me up even more because another film about autism has been released and I've watched the trailer. At first glance it looks like a beautifully made film and then it ends up following the same old tired themes: genius, kooky, loveable kid, always on the outside looking in, eventually discovers his true calling as a maths genius, falls in love with another kooky maths genius and life's twee and isn't-being-autistic-brilliant. And part of me should be delighted and thrilled that it's another celebration of the condition. But it seems so far from the reality we have lived. When will the film be made of the young boy sinking his teeth into his friend's arm or turning round and smacking his parents in the face because sometimes it feels like it's the only way to be heard? That was our experience for so long. Autism isn't this mystical cape that can be unwrapped to reveal an enigma; it is a frightening, horrible, angry, impenetrable fog.

Me and The Boy's mum were just lost in it all. Maybe that's why we still get on now, even after all these years of being separated; it isn't just The Boy who bonds us, it's what we've been through over the years: the finger pointing, the blame. And I've no doubt that parts of the experience exist only in our heads – the sense that we could have done more, could have been more. But it's been said to our faces plenty of times as well. When a child is behaving in a way that no one quite understands, people decide it must be the parents who are at the root of it. They're not strict enough. No boundaries. Next minute they're too strict. Not consistent enough. Then the personal favourite, straight from the 1950s 'Parenting Manual': 'Just bite him back, that'll learn him.' Bite him back. I can't tell you how many times I've heard those words over the years.

In reality, I always hold the knowledge that however strange and distressing we as parents find the situation, I can only imagine how difficult it is for the child caught in the middle of it, the distress and confusion The Boy must feel as he struggles to make sense of the world around him.

Whatever was going on for him internally, it was echoed by his physical presence. The Boy was now four years of age and the promised improvement to his legs hadn't materialized. It seems strange using that phrase now, 'his legs'. It's a phrase still used now, by family, close friends, even The Boy himself. 'My legs' is as much a medical condition as migraine or diabetes. The Boy continued to be so unsteady when he walked or ran. Oh, he could run and run, legs splayed outwards, never quite doing what they were meant to be doing. He'd invariably fall. Every few feet or so, his lack of balance would catch him off-guard and he'd tumble to the ground. Other children of his age might do the same once in a while and then scream and wail with the pain that would mysteriously vanish the minute they felt their mother's hands scoop them to safety. Not The Boy. There were no tears, no crying. The falling down had become as much a part of life as the walking bit. He just got up and carried on.

'Knock-knees. He'll grow out of it.' Another GP appointment over with. The trouble was, no one had ever really got close enough to The Boy to examine him. When you have a boy in your surgery who has been screaming down the waiting room for fifteen minutes under the glaring eye of the gatekeeper behind the reception desk and is currently ripping the paper cover off your bed in the corner of your consultation room, chewing on the small wooden stick normally reserved for moving tongues out of the way for a throat examination, which you handed over in an effort to appease him when he entered, you just want him out of there. At least, that's what it felt like to me.

It became difficult to keep believing 'the legs' were nothing to be concerned about. Wherever we went, playgrounds, soft-play centres, the same conversations. 'What's wrong with his legs?' they'd ask. 'Knock-knees,' I'd reply unconvincingly. 'He'll grow out of it,' I'd add as I hauled him to the top of the slide, The Boy being unable to climb the ladders. Parents looked at me strangely but I was becoming hardened to strange looks by now. Now I realize I spoke to people less and less as time went on. It just became easier to do it that way. No awkward questions I didn't know the answer to.

Deep down, his mum and I knew something wasn't right. 'Carry!' The Boy would plead far too often after walking short distances. 'Carry.' In the end, we decided we needed to know once and for all what was wrong. We made a decision that I can hear my dad tutting at even now. We were desperate, Dad, desperate.

We decided to go private. We paid to see a paediatrician.

Me and Mum both came together for this one – as we'd do for so many appointments over the years. If the struggles in the GP surgery had taught us one thing it was that it needed two of us to get anywhere if there was an appointment with The Boy. In the waiting room one of us could smile sweetly at the gate-keeper and try to convince her you weren't the awful parents she'd already decided you were. The other would try to entertain The Boy with some eighteen-month-old copies of *Amateur Photographer* magazine and *Cosmopolitan* on the table. Then we'd go through to the doctor and we'd maybe reverse the roles. One would do the talking, the other would be the performing clown, the children's entertainer who would try to keep The Boy in the room for long enough for any kind of examination to take place.

The consultant we saw that day was as unremarkable as any other. I tried to convince myself that with the exchange of money she was a bit posher, but in reality she was probably the same consultant we'd have seen on the NHS if we'd ever got a referral.

As we entered the room, Mum took the seat next to her. Dad was hanging on to The Boy, who was already protesting at having to leave his copy of *Cosmopolitan* in the waiting room. It was a small room too, claustrophobic. There wasn't really room for the four of us in there. Wherever the money we'd paid was going, it wasn't on real estate that was for sure.

It is always surprising to think just how much has changed over the last ten years. Nowadays, we go to appointments with iPads, iPhones, headphones and any electronic gadget we can get our hands on. It gets us through things relatively smoothly. Back then, a Nokia 5510 with a game of *Snake* didn't quite cut it. Before those tools were available, medical appointments were a mission, trying to keep The Boy entertained long enough to allow his mum time to tell the consultant what the problem was.

Even if I do say so myself, I've become quite adept over the years at entertaining The Boy. In many ways it is no different to performing for punters in comedy clubs. When you first start, you're unsure of your audience and, when you get it wrong, sometimes they just sit and stare at you. Other times they're far more vocal in their dislike for what you're doing. But the more you do it, the more you find your way. The laughs become more regular, the periods where you get it really wrong become rarer. The Boy, like all children, was one of the most candid audiences I've ever had. Children don't bother with niceties or worry about coming across as rude if they don't find you funny. There's an honesty that's by turns both refreshing and brutal. Nowadays, the tables have turned and The Boy makes me laugh just as much as I do him. We share the same sense of humour, we laugh at the same things. And hearing him laugh, a proper full-on laugh where he clutches his stomach and makes little shrieking noises as he struggles to catch his breath, are my favourite moments.

They're still the bits that will forever mean more than any standing ovation in London's West End. Not that I'd know what that feels like, but you get the idea.

I have a hefty back catalogue of Desperate Dad's Compendium of Childish Games to Entertain the Bored and Indifferent. Different games for different occasions that we've adapted, learnt and mastered between the two of us over the years to get us through sticky situations. Here are a couple of the old favourites, although I have a sneaking suspicion these may well fall in to the 'you had to be there' category. Let's see.

If we're outdoors and The Boy is getting tired and restless, there's Park Keeper. All we need is some grass (that's the Park bit). And an adult (that's the Keeper). The Park Keeper is a grumpy man with a strange, pirate-like accent (OK, it's the only one I can do). Park Keeper doesn't like children on his grass. In fact, if the Keeper catches any children on the grass, he will shout, 'GET OFF MY GRASS!', chase the offender, pick them up and throw them over his shoulder and put them in the 'tool shed' (normally a drain cover they have to stand on). If playing with more than one child, they can tag each other to get out of the tool shed. If there is just one child playing, they can escape when the Park Keeper turns his back to do some weeding.

Master the basics of Park Keeper and you can then move on to Park Keeper Advanced. This involves various adaptations to the original version that The Boy has crafted over the years. Animals are now allowed on the grass or, more specifically, cows, chicken or sheep, as The Boy can make the noises for each of them. If the Park Keeper hears an animal on his grass, he will leave them to graze, but he needs to keep his wits about him because if one of the animals suddenly talks, then the Park Keeper, using his powers of deduction, will realize that it isn't a real animal but is instead a small child *pretending to be* an animal. Park Keeper will stop in his tracks. He will stare at the animal, daring to make a sound, as little excited giggles emit from the animal's mouth. Slowly, Park Keeper will scratch his head, and then utter the climactic words, 'Wait-a-minute… Chickens-can't-talk. You're-not-a-chicken. You're-a… child! GET OFF MY GRASS!' And then it's off to the tool shed, as in the original game.

Park Keeper is without doubt The Boy's favourite game of all time. We've played it with cousins, on holidays, in the park and at school; anywhere a distraction has been needed, Park Keeper has been there.

I don't mind telling you, I'm pretty proud of this game we created together that has shaped so many family outings and days out. Yet it's only now that I've written it down for the first time that I see it is little more than picking my son up and putting him down again on a different spot. I don't think Mattel will be bringing out the board game version just yet.

I've just told The Boy that I've included Park Keeper in the book. And all he said was, 'What about Ride of Your Life?' So, at his request, here we go with the second offering from Desperate Dad's Compendium of Childish Games to Entertain the Bored and Indifferent. This particular game has been through many upgrades over the years to become the current market leader. Ladies and gentlemen, I present: Ride of Your Life!

For this game we will need to be indoors, preferably on the carpet. To prepare, clear an area of approximately ten foot square in the lounge. Remove any nearby breakables (fortunately enough, having lived with The Boy, these have been smashed some time before anyway). Now, to play. Dad lies flat on his front on the floor in the middle of the lounge. The Boy then sits on Dad's back (over the years, the largely involuntary sound Dad makes as his chest is squashed against the floor by the weight of his child bearing down on him has grown louder and more involuntary). Then, the ride begins to speak in a gravelly voice (with a hint of pirate, naturally). It is Dad's finest performance since he was thrown out of drama school all those years ago.

'Welcome. To. Ride. Of. Your. Life. Prepare yourself for the ride of a lifetime. Warning, this ride is only suitable for riders over the age of eighteen. Prepare to be scared. Very scared.'

At this point Dad raises himself up so he's now on his hands and knees with the child on his back. (If you're really good, and this is something I'd only really recommend to advanced players, make mechanical sounds simultaneously.) The ride continues to speak. Maybe in a Richard Burton kind of voice. 'You now must make your ride selection. Please state clearly your ride choice, from one to one hundred.'

The Boy always chooses ride six.

'You have selected ride six. Ride six is the Tyrannosaurus Rex ride. Please fasten your seatbelt. The ride will begin in three seconds. Three… two… one…' And then just bounce up and down, flinging the child around and around. Once they've been flung off, the ride comes to an end, and Dad flops back to lying on the floor again.

'Welcome. To. Ride…'

In the multiplayer version there are variations for different cousins and friends. Ride forty-four is the *Ben 10* ride, after the TV series. Ride seventeen the Barbie ride. Ride sixty-seven is Power Rangers. None of them ever went quite as fast as ride six though. Without even realizing it, Dad always seemed to work that bit harder for ride six.

Anyway, I digress too much. The consulting room which we were in that day, when we went to see the paediatrician, was small. Far too small for Ride of Your Life. And there was no patch of grass for Park Keeper either. Instead, I produced a picture book from my bag – old school. Reading a whole book from cover to cover could tide us over for at least as long as forty-seven seconds. The Boy loved books or, rather, he liked turning pages. No words, they just caused confusion. He had no interest whatsoever in them and their confusing shapes, and he certainly didn't have time to sit around while I read them out loud. I'm not even sure he ever really liked the pictures. He just seemed to like the motion of turning the pages. Maybe it was a sensory thing of feeling the air across his face as the pages turned, calming, soothing. Maybe it was the familiarity of something from home in an unfamiliar place. Or maybe his dad is reading too much into the situation again and he just wanted to get to the end of the bloody book and out of the room away from the woman who is sitting too close and keeps talking and talking.

By the time the consultant came to examine his legs, The Boy was in full-scale meltdown. As she reached down to try to manipulate them to get some sense of the difficulties he had, The Boy leant over and sank his teeth into her arm. Examination over.

'Well, you need to sort out his behaviour before you do anything else,' she said.

'What about his legs?' we asked, as we were bundled out of the door.

'Knock-knees,' she said without even looking up from the computer screen as she inputted her findings for the invoice. 'He'll grow out of it.'

CHAPTER THIRTEEN

The Best Days of Your Life

Once upon a time The Boy went to school with The Boy Who Couldn't Sit Still. The Boy Who Couldn't Sit Still didn't really like school. In fact he hated it. Too many rules. Too much pressure to conform. He forever seemed to be on overdrive, as if he operated on a completely different wavelength to everyone else. His fists and his mouth would react to situations long before his brain even had time to engage.

The Boy Who Couldn't Sit Still was half the size of the other children, I nicknamed him Dash, after the son in *The Incredibles*. And he was nothing short of incredible. I have never seen a child move so quickly, darting out of the classroom and on to the roof before anyone could react. He liked the roof. A lot. I'm not sure if it was the sense of danger or the fact that the teachers would never dare follow him up there. All I know is whenever I used to go and collect The Boy, The Boy Who Couldn't Sit Still always appeared most content when he was out of reach of the world.

One day, I went into school and nine fire doors had been kicked in. Nine. Those thick glass panes with the wire inside. It was The Boy Who Couldn't Sit Still. Four-foot-something of destruction had unleashed his anger with mankind. And it was probably because he didn't want to wash his hands before lunch or queue up after break.

The Boy Who Couldn't Sit Still's mum would come to collect him. We crossed paths regularly – I'd have been phoned to collect my son for some misdemeanour or other and, as I pulled up into the car park, she'd be calling hers down from the roof. She was exhausted. He didn't sleep at night, only for a couple of hours. She had nothing but my full admiration.

You see, The Boy Who Couldn't Sit Still was diagnosed with ADHD. You know the one – that supposedly non-existent condition caused by crap parents that people snigger about. Well, I'm no expert but I remember when I worked in a respite care home for children with disabilities for a couple of years. Originally I worked there to help put The Boy and his problems into perspective. And then I stayed because I loved it. And the most challenging children, the ones who struggled to fit in the most, were often those whose diagnoses included ADHD. Yet still people mock it as a condition or say it's just spoilt children with appalling parents.

So, in some ways The Boy and I are lucky. Autism is becoming more and more recognized. If you go on Facebook or Twitter, every other day seems to be Autism Day for one reason or another. And don't get me wrong, I'm eternally grateful for that. But let's spare a thought for those who have conditions that aren't as well recognized. I was used to being labelled a Shit Parent before The Boy was diagnosed. His diagnosis helped deal with that a lot. I can't imagine what it must be like when, even after diagnosis, the label sticks.

Before I get down off my soapbox, I'd just like to declare today ADHD Wednesday. Join The Boy Who Couldn't Sit Still and shout it from the rooftops.

MY SON'S NOT RAINMAN BLOG

I can't remember the exact moment the 'Shitty Parent' label was first applied. Its use certainly increased after The Boy started school.

It began as a whisper or an overheard conversation. Then it might be included in a discussion around 'boundaries' that also involved a plastic 'caring' smile. Periodically the term might be joined by the 'Munchausen parent' label, especially if I challenged or questioned decisions too much.

A few weeks ago I was attending a parenting course (I told you I was no expert) and if there was one consistent factor among those parents present, it was that all of us had been labelled the same thing at some point or other over the years.

I've tried to shake it off but it always rears its head in one form or another – the constant nagging insinuation that I haven't done enough, haven't *been* enough. I've been too busy fooling around playing Park Keeper and Ride of Your Life or teaching The Boy to say, 'Have a break, have a Kwik Krap,' in a Liverpool accent when I should have been fighting the system, insisting on second opinions or banging down doors for intervention.

And so to school. By the time The Boy had been offered a place at the local primary school, to start in January, we had been through two nurseries and a childminder and sensed it wasn't going to be an easy ride. There was a small private school nearby with just fifteen pupils to a class. It was half the price of most of the other private options. They would take him from September and we could see how he got on. The money was about the same as we were paying for the nursery and we could afford it between the two of us, couldn't we? Couldn't we? I'll pack in the fags, that'll help.

With all this talk of private medical consultations and schools, I don't want to paint the picture of us as an affluent family throwing an endless amount of money at our problems. The truth is I was on my arse, financially, and I suspect we both were. Mum was paying for a house that was too big and I was paying for a flat I could ill afford. But we were also desperate. Desperate to try to find the right place for him. If he got off to the right start in a small school, we could put everything that had happened up to that point behind us. His dad had been unwell, his parents had separated, it was just the upheaval that was causing the difficulties. We'd manage. I bought a crappy old Rover 214 off eBay with a credit card so I could get him to school. Grandparents helped out with the uniform. This was it, we were off. An awfully big adventure. School.

Six weeks he lasted. Six long, painful weeks. We'd met the class teacher before and she was very sweet and kind, in her last year of teaching at the end of an illustrious career before retirement. Think Mrs Doubtfire without the five o'clock shadow. At the end of day one, she gave me a thumbs-up when I went to collect him. All had gone well – we'd forewarned her of the problems that might lie ahead, but she seemed confident. Almost happy, even.

Day two came around, another thumbs-up, although I thought I detected a slight downturn in the smile. Stop it, John. Everything is fine.

Day three, Mum collected him, there was no thumbs-up. Maybe she was just busy, distracted.

Day four, she didn't make eye contact and by day five there was a note in the home-school diary: Can we have a quick meeting on Monday at home time, please?

The quick meeting involved the deputy head and the teacher. They asked how things had been at home. They'd been OK, we said. He was tired with being at school all day, but he was doing OK. How were things at school? There was a bit of a pause. They'd never had anyone like him before and they were unsure what to do. For one brief moment, I swelled with pride. An enigma, you say? But, no. The Boy refused to participate in anything. He screamed. He threw things. He bit people. He hit out. He disrupted the teaching for the others. He didn't wait his turn. He refused to line up. He was unsteady on the stairs. The list went on. They were going to persevere, though. He'd been through some changes at home, maybe he'd settle in a couple of weeks. Perhaps he was bored being at the back of the class. They'd give him a seat at the front, near the teacher. Don't worry, everything is fine.

One week later, another meeting. 'We've requested an educational psychologist to visit from the local authority. We're just waiting for them to confirm. We should hear in the next couple of weeks.'

We never got as far as meeting the educational psychologist, at least not on this occasion. It would be another year before we crossed her path. 'We aren't the right setting for him,' they smiled kindly, at the end of yet another meeting. 'I'm afraid we can't meet his needs.'

It's too painful looking back to even try to consider what impact each and every exclusion had on The Boy. He did have difficulty making and maintaining friendships, there's no doubt, but in each setting he certainly did have friends – maybe not in the conventional sense in those early days, maybe they were just allies to play *alongside* rather than *with*. But to him, I have no doubt, they were friends, people he liked who were continually removed from his life. And the worry was, this was a class of fifteen children. The next step was to go back to the local primary school with thirty-two children. How would they cope?

It was only November and as the new school wasn't going to take him until January, we had to sort out childcare. By this point it had become obvious to me and Mum that both of us holding down full-time jobs was next to impossible. It wasn't really a difficult decision to make – Mum had a career, a job she'd worked towards for many years; I, on the other hand, very much just had a job. And after the long period of sickness, I reckoned secretly they'd be only too happy to let me go. They were. I had a good employer and an amazing boss who came up with a redundancy package that meant I could get through the next few months at least. By now we'd implemented our shared care arrangement (ugh, how clinical does that sound?) and The Boy was spending every other week at my flat. I'd just have him in the daytime as well for a while. I could look for a new job once he settled at the next school, when things would be much calmer…

We got on fine in those couple of months, the two of us adapting to days of Park Keeper and Ride of Your Life. It felt good, after being unwell for so long, to be able to prove that I could do it, if not to anyone else then to myself. Parenting.

Before long, January came around. School number two and we weren't even out of reception class. A new uniform, new friends to make but maybe, just maybe… a new start. Me and Mum went along to meet the new teacher, Miss A. I liked her the first moment I met her. She was newly qualified, straight out of teacher training and had a gentleness about her that I knew The Boy would love. Then I met her sidekick, a ferocious teaching assistant who terrified the life out of me. Good cop, bad cop. Maybe they'd be the perfect team.

Within a fortnight, I'd been asked to go in to school at lunchtimes to support The Boy (the choice was either that or bring him home for lunch). So many parents have since told me I should have refused, that I should have let the school deal with things on their own. That way the school would have to bring in additional help if they felt it was necessary. Looking back, I know those parents were absolutely right but at the time I was desperate to try to ensure another placement didn't break down before it had even properly started.

I don't regret going in to the school at lunchtime though. Maybe it was just what I needed to appreciate how hard things were for him – it gave me so much insight, watching him trying to interact with others in a huge playground. I've often thought it's a luxury most parents don't get, to see the child in their own environment, away from the security of home and to see just how they engage with the world.

Lunchtimes and playtimes were the worst time for him, with the lack of a routine and free-play stretching ahead. I was able to see just how much of a struggle school was and how hard he found it to communicate with other children, much preferring actions and gestures to make himself be heard.

I'd never noticed before just how much children communicate without words all the time. As adults, we're rubbish at it. We might have a couple of hand gestures up our sleeve for when a car pulls out in front of us, but apart from that and the universal mime of signing-the-chequebook-in-mid-air-when-asking-for-the-bill, we don't have much else in the repertoire.

Children have 'tag' (or 'tig', depending on where you are in the world). For so long it was The Boy's gateway to reaching other people. And the best bit of it all was that no words were required. He'd walk up to a child in a playground, tag them and run off. Some wouldn't get it, but that was OK. It was bit like speed-dating for children – they just move on and tag the next person. Eventually someone will get it and, once that other child turns to run after you to tag you back, that's it. You've cracked the code. Friends.

These friendships were often short-lived. Once the other child had tagged The Boy, the game was over. There would be no reciprocal chase. The Boy would head off to find someone else to do it all over again with. He was only ever interested in being hunted. Maybe he felt important that way. Maybe even at that young age he'd already spent so long trying to fit in that some-one chasing him made him feel wanted, made him feel like he belonged. Or maybe his dad should stop trying to romanticize a story about two kids legging it around a playground.

Apart from just watching The Boy though, I started to get a sense for schools and how they worked. Maybe that's another reason every parent should spend a day in a school. Not only to see how their own perfect little sunbeam really behaves, but also to get a sense of just how difficult a task teaching can be. When you start to think about it, school is such a strange concept. It's the only time in our lives when we are forced to sit in one room with thirty other people for years on end, being forced to get along when the only thing we have in common is that we were all born in the same twelve-month period.

There were so many rules and regulations that The Boy just found utterly confusing. He hated standing in line. I understand it can be difficult to get thirty-two five-year-olds to walk in an orderly fashion to assembly, but the standing-in-line business was a real eye-opener to me. Children were made to line up to go to the toilet, the playground, to breathe. I kind of understand why – when you have so many children in your care, if you don't instil certain rules then there is the danger that anarchy will ensue. But I have also noticed over the years that there's a direct correlation between how much the school wants children to stand in lines and how crap it is. The worst schools – and, let's face it, we've been through a few – seem to be the ones trying to create their own Foreign Legion, where conformity and lining up mean far more than creativity and expression ever will.

Oh, how arty-farty and liberal of me. Really, I'm bound to say that, given I have the child who refuses to line up. Looking back now at those lunchtimes, maybe it wasn't the free time and lack of routine that caused The Boy so many problems. Maybe it was the lining up. Line up to leave the classroom, line up to go and wash your hands, line up to enter the hall, line up to collect your lunch, line up to put your tray away, line up to leave the hall, line up to enter the playground, it just went on. It took the school over twelve months to finally realize that if they took him out of line then the scratching, hitting and biting stopped.

At first, the SENCO (Special Educational Needs Coordinator) told me that my son was just 'bloody-minded'. That he always wanted to be at the front of the line, he was spoilt and was just trying to get his own way. But for The Boy it was never about being at the front of the line. All he wanted to do was avoid the middle. The middle of the line was awful, with people in close proximity – crammed in, claustrophobic. Nowhere to go, no escape. Just people. Everywhere. With their noises and smells and breath. Awful, terrifying people. Trapped front and back.

For the whole school year The Boy was forced to stand in lines. He didn't have the words to tell people it *hurt*. Physically hurt. So he did what our instinct teaches us to do when we feel cornered and vulnerable; he hit out, went wild. The urge to protect himself kicked in. And he learnt that if he kept hitting out then people wouldn't make him stand in line anymore. He didn't hit out to hurt people; he hit out to make his own pain go away. And he hit out because it was the only way he could make himself heard.

One day Miss A suggested to The Boy that he stand at the back of the line. That was the day the hitting stopped. He could dawdle a bit, put some space between himself and the other children. He could breathe again. And the pain went away.

And I remember all this because I often wonder, if someone had reached him sooner, helped to identify his problems at a younger age, how much easier would The Boy have found things? I'm quite ashamed to admit it now, but I also remember in those early days secretly wanting a child who would just follow the others, who would stand in line, who'd conform and do things without the outbursts, quirky behaviours and strange noises.

Nowadays though, I'm incredibly proud that The Boy will forever dance to a different beat. And surely that can only be a good thing. Children shouldn't always be made to stand in line and conform. They have a lifetime of that ahead. Let them find themselves first. And once they have, let them run free awhile – the school bell will wait for one more day.

CHAPTER FOURTEEN

Play Away

The other day I took The Boy to the snappily named Children and Young People Development Centre. It's a one-stop shop where you go to address all your concerns about your child's wellbeing – health, social care and education – under one award-winningly designed, eco-friendly roof with garish coloured windows.

Chances are you'll know someone in there, having met them at an occupational therapy class or at some support group or another. On the whole, I like meeting other parents. It's good to listen and share with those who know and understand. But here was the shocker to me: some of them are arseholes.

There are arseholes the world over, I get that, but for some reason I thought this sacred group were exempt. But, no, it turns out that proportionately it's the same as everywhere else – a percentage of parents of children with special needs are arseholes.

When I sat down the other day in the reception area (we're so focused on the children with our coloured windows), I spotted a woman and her son from a physiotherapy class. 'Fancy seeing you here,' I said joking. I'm ever so witty like that. Then it started.

'We're never out of here. We might as well move in. This is the third time this month. They've never seen anyone like him,' she blurted out. And as her rant gathered momentum I realized that it was too late. I found myself unwittingly playing yet another game of Disability Top Trumps.

To explain, Disability Top Trumps is a game played by some parents who will try to outdo the 'disabledness' of your child with their own and turn it into a kind of a competition:

'Oh, your Jessica sleeps for three hours a night? Well, I'm lucky if James here manages an hour…'

'…it takes you fifty-five minutes to get ready for school each morning? That's nothing, we have to start getting ready the day before…'

'…I'll see your feeding tube and raise you epilepsy and challenging behaviour…'

Disability Top Trumps. I'm not sure why people do it. Or maybe I am. I recognize that some are purely venting their frustrations. But sometimes it seems to be more than that. We all want our children to be the very best at things; we all want them to thrive and succeed. And when realization hits that your child won't be the captain of the first XI or soloist in the school orchestra, some people have to find something that their child can be top of, even if that means claiming the best-at-being-disabled crown.

I know this all sounds a bit harsh. And it probably says more about me and my inadequacies than about others. Who am I to moan about my problems when other people have far worse to deal with? There's plenty who have been dealt a worse hand than me.

All I know is, I hate playing Disability Top Trumps. So if you're one of those who do it, please stop. I've had parents come up to me after the show and state that they feel like a fraud because their child 'is only a bit autistic' or apologizing because their children 'aren't that bad'. This whole thing isn't a competition. Just for once, can't everyone be a winner?

MY SON'S NOT RAINMAN BLOG

Monday morning, 9.45 a.m. Play therapy. Children and Young People Development Centre. I think this was the first time we ever stepped foot in the building. Strange to imagine a world without it and what it contains – paediatricians, therapists, psychiatrists, psychologists, health visitors, social workers, nurses, special educational needs teams, they're all here. The idea being that all the departments work together closely, sharing clinics and information.

That first time we walked in there, The Boy aged five, I had no idea how much time we'd end up spending in the building over the years, how many of its meeting and consulting rooms we'd sit in, how many different floors I'd visit or how many letters marked 'Urgent – by hand' I'd pass over the front desk. Even now, it continues to feature in our lives on at least a weekly basis. I might bemoan the system at times, but maybe it's a reminder that in some ways we're fortunate – the help is there. Often it's finding it that can be the difficult part.

It's funny, really, the lottery of life, how for some families it will only ever be another anonymous building they drive past on the way to school each morning, not even sure what its purpose is; for others it is central to the landscape of their lives. Good news, bad news, most of it emanated from here.

But on that Monday morning, our first visit, I wasn't sure what to expect – my own experiences of therapy up until that point had made me sceptical, to say the least. Since coming out of hospital I'd seen a number of practitioners, each keen to take advantage of my employer's generous health insurance. There had been Samantha, an incredibly posh lady with an office on Baker Street in central London who possessed what seemed to be an unhealthy obsession with my relationship with my mum; there was Martin who said he saw a lot of people from up north because they all grew up in terraced houses and the close proximity to each other was incredibly stressful; and then there was Graeme, a man whose entire wardrobe was made up of different shades of brown, who would sit cross-legged on his chair and say absolutely nothing every session until I spoke. Instead of speaking, Graeme used to make little guttural sounds at the back of his throat every minute or so. I'm not by nature a violent man, but I can't tell you how close I came to hitting Graeme.

Well, it turned out the play therapist was a Frances, a cheerful Irish woman who I warmed to instantly. Sometimes I meet people and start to ponder why they do the job they do. But when I meet someone like Frances, I can tell right away it's because they love it. She met us at reception and walked us upstairs to the meeting room. Upon entering we saw that across the back wall were a range of toys all laid out. The Boy made a beeline for them straight away, with me and his mum pulling him back, ready with the 'Don't touch' that was always on the tip of our tongue. 'Don't touch' accompanied us on every aisle in the supermarket, echoed round the walls of friends' houses and bounced off every surface of a waiting room. 'Don't touch,' invariably followed by the action of trying to prise open a small fist clenched around whatever item was foolish enough to leave itself within his reach. We'd become quite good at it over the years – The Boy's mum had much better reflexes than me, but every now and then I'd manage to get hold of that porcelain goldfish before it made it into his mouth.

'He's fine,' Frances said, 'let him be. It gives me an opportunity to get some background from you.'

'I'm going to talk with Mummy and Daddy for a little bit,' she explained, 'you can play with any of the toys you want to.'

The Boy lurched forward to the toys; being given carte blanche to get stuck in was a novelty. He proceeded to pick up a crocodile puppet. Instinctively he placed his hand inside it and then, moving his hand up and down to open and close its mouth, he used it to bash and bite every other toy while making growling noises. Frances made no comment, instead observing him continuously as she asked me and Mum the same old questions everyone asked on a first appointment.

'Any complications during the pregnancy?'

'What about the birth?'

'And when did you first start having concerns?'

'When did he first talk?'

'Walk?'

'Any family history of mental illness?'

The Boy had been playing on his own for a few minutes and the growling noises he was making were getting louder and louder. The crocodile had now wiped every other toy off the table, and although the shark put up a bit of a fight it finally joined the rest in toy Armageddon, scattered across the floor. The Boy looked up, crocodile still firmly in place, and seemed to suddenly remember that the three of us were also in the room. Playtime was over: it was time to turn his attention to the adults.

Here in the UK there's quite a famous clip featuring chat show host Michael Parkinson. His show went out in the 1970s and it was all very civilized and British. Guests chatted about their latest film, drank their whisky and smoked their cigarettes. One of those guests was a man called Rod Hull, a puppeteer whose character was an emu called, somewhat originally, Emu. It's probably politest to describe Rod Hull as 'eccentric'. Emu the bird-puppet-thing under Rod Hull's nominal control kept interrupting the conversation and trying to bite Michael Parkinson in the face in a very un-British way. The audience went wild. Well, if you've seen that interview you pretty much know what happened in the rest of that play therapy session, minus the appreciative audience and with a large crocodile puppet in place of the malevolent Emu. Was it because we were talking about The Boy? Maybe. Or perhaps it was just the noise of people talking that he found so difficult. Whatever it was, he clambered between the three of us, the crocodile launching at our faces, trying to close our mouths or grabbing us by the arm, with the small human hand beneath the fabric teeth twisting our skin as it grabbed.

'The crocodile is very angry,' Frances commented calmly, seemingly unfazed by any of it. 'I don't think the crocodile likes to be ignored. Maybe Dad would like to play with the crocodile for a while?' Oh, Dad can think of nothing more he'd rather do. I left her and Mum to carry on filling in our chequered history and I took my place next to The Boy at the toy table. He calmed down a little and, between the two of us, we created some sort of game. I picked up the toys that had been thrown on the floor, the crocodile bit them or hit them with the top of his head and then threw them on the floor again. I picked them back up and passed them to the crocodile.

We had four sessions with Frances. Each session would begin the same way with the toys lined up and The Boy helping himself. Over time I realized that the toys weren't just placed randomly on that table; there was thought given to it, an order. Even the initial selection of toys had a purpose. And each time The Boy did exactly the same thing – he burst into the room, took the crocodile puppet, placed it on his hand and then attacked every other toy until they were all on the floor. Then once again he'd turn his attention to the adults.

Whatever he did, Frances didn't reprimand him for it. Instead, she started to give a commentary on what he was doing, to put his actions into words.

'The crocodile is making lots of noise today. He's biting a lot. The crocodile has thrown the woman and the boy away. Now he's biting the dinosaur's neck. The crocodile is trying to bite Dad's arm. Now he's biting Frances. He's trying to bite Frances's mouth.'

Then she started to colour in the rest of the story, to speculate on how the crocodile felt and what his motives might be.

'I don't think the crocodile likes it when people talk about biting. The crocodile seems very angry with everyone. I wonder what is making him angry? The crocodile thinks nobody under-stands him and he gets frightened sometimes. And when he gets frightened, that can make him angry. But the crocodile wants to be friends with people. He likes having friends. Being angry all the time can be very lonely. But he doesn't know how to make friends. The crocodile doesn't really like biting. He bites when he wants things to stop. He bites when he's scared. He bites because he doesn't have any words to say how he really feels.'

I can't do it justice here, the impact of those sessions – it just seems like a load of mumbo-jumbo when I write it down. The effect on The Boy was extraordinary. Within four weeks, the crocodile became calmer. He bit less. He even used to rest his head on Dad's arm and wait for it to be stroked. He made friends with the shark and, by the end of the session, more toys would remain on the table than the previous week. I was a convert – the time we spent with Frances gave us insight, a way to The Boy that we just hadn't had before. That phrase came back to me again, 'All behaviour is a form of communication,' but never was it made more clear than during those sessions. For years I had been waiting for The Boy to tell me how he felt, to explain to me what was going on. It turned out he'd been telling me all along; I just hadn't known how to listen.

For the fifth session, Frances asked if she could see me and Mum alone. She just wanted to discuss how the sessions were going and how we felt things were moving forward. It was the same room but without The Boy and the toys laid out on the table, but it couldn't have been more different – eerie. Three solitary chairs and four bare walls with nothing but a laminated poster, above the light switch, detailing what to do in the event of a fire. Only the quiet hum of traffic outside filled the silence where the crocodile used to be.

Frances had some concerns. She felt that while The Boy was making real progress, there were many behaviours he was exhibiting that were beyond her scope as a play therapist. She wanted to get another opinion. She had made a referral to the autism clinic. In the meantime, she said, it wasn't in The Boy's best interests to continue the sessions, not until a proper diagnosis had been made.

We left in silence. It was difficult for me and his mum, going into appointments together and then leaving separately afterwards. No one to talk things through with. And all we had between us was that word, 'autism'. First mentioned by my brother, it had been said in whispers a few time since then but now here it was once more, loudly filling the gap where normally The Boy would have been.

My thoughts were interrupted by my mobile phone ringing.

'John? It's Jackie, from the school. There's been another incident. We're going to have to exclude him again. Can you come to collect him, please? Sarah feels a meeting with you and Mum might be useful.'

Oh crocodile, one day we'll find a way to put all of this into words.

CHAPTER FIFTEEN

Let's Add a Label to It

Andy Murray, Britain's finest tennis player since seemingly forever, won another tournament on Sunday. I tried to get The Boy interested. I told him that Great Britain won. He couldn't have cared less though, because he doesn't live in Great Britain. He lives in London.

I like that The Boy has no sporting allegiances. I find it really refreshing. We went to a football match last year and he decided which team he was going to support when we got there. He picked the blue one. When they changed ends at half time he switched to the red one.

The least successful sporting event we tried was the 2012 Paralympics in London. Oh, the irony! By this stage the wheelchair featured far more in our lives than it had done before so Dad decided to book tickets for the wheelchair basketball. Dad had decided that it would be a positive display of disability that would fill The Boy with hope and courage for the future. Sometimes, Dad makes really stupid decisions.

We arrived at the huge venue on the banks of the river Thames, resplendent in our Great Britain colours. We had a good view of the court from the wheelchair-viewing area; we unfurled our Union Jack flag and it was hung with pride from the balcony. Then we waited. And waited. For an hour. By the time the basketball started, the iPad had been exhausted and the drink/eat/toilet card had been played too early. Dad could feel this one slipping through his fingers.

Wheelchair basketball is an amazing sport. It's fast and furious. And very, very loud. It's accompanied by upbeat music, flashing lights, people shouting and it's played indoors – unlike a football match there is no open sky for the sound to dissipate into. It hits the roof of the stadium and rains back down on you. Six minutes we lasted. For The Boy they were six, long, painful minutes.

The hitting out was subtle at first. Then, as the sensory overload reached critical levels, so did the behaviour. Pinching, scratching, screaming. I decided to make a run for it. Grateful that we'd brought the wheelchair, I wheeled him out of the stadium into the area outside. By then he was out of control, trying to hit me any way he could, desperate to bite, to hit, to scratch, anything. I thought being away from the basketball would make things better, but it just seemed to make them worse.

By this point, two security guards had arrived. They stood to one side, not sure what to do, watching. And to them it must have looked like a grown man was having a fight with a boy in a wheelchair. I pushed onwards, thinking the further away from the noise we got the more The Boy would settle. He didn't. He was flinging his arms at me, filled with a rage I hadn't seen before, even by his standards. And all the time we were followed by security. Just watching. Radios in hand.

The further away we walked the more agitated The Boy became. Security were now calling for back-up. I thought the police would be called, which sounds very dramatic but it's very hard – when someone is hitting you and just wants you to go away, but you can't leave them alone for their own safety and you just don't know what to do.

Then along came one of those heroes of the Olympic Games. The volunteers who make it all happen. And I thought, here we go, a do-gooder. He smiled at me and then knelt down next to The Boy's wheelchair. 'What's the matter?' he said to him calmly. 'Can I help you?' His face was in perfect reach for The Boy. I was about to warn him he'd better move when suddenly The Boy stopped screaming and looked at him.

'My flag,' he said.

Then it dawned on me. We'd left the flag tied to the balcony. And so the volunteer did his own sprint down the corridor and moments later returned victorious with the Union Jack flapping in his hands.

'Thank you,' The Boy said.

And just like that, it was over. There were many reports in the newspapers that it was the volunteers who had made the London 2012 games such a success and every one of them was correct.

We quietly went home and sat on the sofa to watch the rest of the basketball on the television with the sound turned down and the Union Jack flag draped across our legs.

The red team won.

MY SON'S NOT RAINMAN BLOG

The appointment came through for the autism clinic. It would be with a consultant paediatrician and a speech and language therapist. We were to allow two and a half hours.

I can't remember what emotions were coursing through us as we sat in the waiting area that morning. I'd started reading up about autism once again and there was still so much that didn't match The Boy. Yes there was development delay, but he didn't line his toys up, he didn't walk on tip-toes and he certainly didn't prefer his own company. Here was someone desperate to interact with others; he just hadn't got the instruction book.

We filed into the room and this time there were four of us. The Boy had been in his school for around nine months and, as well as me supporting him at lunchtime, he now had a one-to-one teaching assistant in the classroom who had come along too. She knew his struggles better than anyone and she also knew he would find it hard to cope with such a long assessment without some respite now and again. She became an important part of the family in those days.

As usual, the Boy burst into the room like a whirlwind. His time in play therapy had led him to believe that behind every door in the building were tables filled with toys. He scanned his surroundings, spotted a cupboard in the corner that might well contain something interesting and sat down in front of it. The room was much larger than the last consulting room, with a two-way mirror across one wall. After initial introductions, the speech and language therapist took her place next to The Boy to play, his teaching assistant already trying to return the contents of the cupboard to their shelves. The Boy ignored the new faces, as he did most people he didn't know on a first meeting. The paediatrician sat down with me and Mum and asked the same old questions once more.

'Any complications during the pregnancy?'

'What about the birth?'

'And when did you first start having concerns?'

'When did he first talk?'

'Walk?'

'Any family history of mental illness?'

She paused for a while on the last question. I hated talking about it, wanted to get past it and on with our lives but, even here in this room, it still overshadowed everything.

There was a link, she explained, between autism in a child and bipolar disorder in a parent. The research was patchy but there was no doubt it existed. I nodded – Google had already told me that, but I'd put it to the back of my mind until now.

She continued to ask about schooling, nursery, behaviour, routines. Every now and then we'd be joined by The Boy, trying to drag one of us to the corner of the room where he dominated the games being played. It all seemed strange, almost wrong – here we all were discussing him, yet he had no clue as to what any of it was about. Even the games he was encouraged to play were diagnostic tests attempting to discover just how his mind worked.

Halfway through the session, the two professionals swapped roles. The paediatrician headed over to play with The Boy while the speech and language therapist sat with me and Mum. More questions; around excessive dribbling, sound formation, repetitive phrases. We went on too much with some of the answers – the chance to talk endlessly about the one person we loved more than anything meant we became carried away. I noticed it all the time in meetings with staff at school and with healthcare professionals – their eyes would begin to glaze over as we told them the story about a funny thing that happened once when our son was trying to cut a sausage with a spoon. Parents, we don't know when to stop.

By this point The Boy had had enough. Being confined in one room, even with toys to play with, was just too much. His voice was becoming louder from the corner. I could hear his teaching assistant trying to calm him. He started to move away from the corner where he'd played for so long. As if discovering the rest of the room for the first time, he noticed the door we'd walked through earlier. A way out.

I got to the door at about the same time he did. He had been so close and yet so far. The frustration just spilled out of him. The Boy was desperate to get out of that room. He became distressed and angry, tears of rage spilling down his cheeks. Like a deep-sea diver suddenly deprived of his oxygen tank, the panic in his eyes was all too real. It all became too much and he sank his teeth into my arm.

I suppose I should have felt relief that the professionals had witnessed the behaviour that had been so difficult to manage. Me, his mum, even the poor teaching assistant, we'd all been bitten so often, it had just become a part of our lives. And here it was for them to see. And then once he'd bitten, it was like the life force drained out of him. He became docile, compliant – often after a meltdown he'd sleep, the effort it took to maintain that level of ferocity taking it out of him.

After what seemed like forever, the professionals finished their assessment. They now wanted to go away for a few minutes and discuss their findings. The Boy was calm. His teaching assistant nipped out for a cigarette while he and I played 'Scooby-Doo' in the corner, forever grateful that his mum had packed his favourite figures in her bag as an emergency back-up. That was life with The Boy, each pocket filled with a little something that might buy you a few extra minutes or even seconds when it all got too much. A carton of drink. Breadsticks. Power Rangers.

I kept glancing up at the mirror across the wall. Were they behind there, looking in, making their decision? Or were they in the smoking area outside, laughing and joking before flipping a coin to decide the outcome? It was such a surreal few minutes. There was no blood test that could give us the answer, no brain scan. They weren't going to come in and place an x-ray on the light box above the desk and discuss their findings. They were just two people having a chat before they decided whether or not my child had a major brain developmental condition. They came back in and sat down.

I'd only really had one other experience of hearing significant medical news from a professional, years ago, when I was told by a nurse that my dad's cancer was terminal. My mum knew but bottled telling me, deciding it was easier to let it come from the nursing staff. I don't blame her really, she'd have only worded it badly, wanting to get the message across but at the same time wanting to protect her offspring. We were in a small room at the end of the ward where it was quiet. 'I'm sorry,' he said. 'I'll leave you alone with your thoughts for a few minutes. I'll be right outside if you need me, just take your time.' It was that quietness I remember the most.

This time was different. I had Shaggy and The Boy had Scooby-Doo. Velma, Freddy and Daphne were round the other side of the cupboard. We were running from monsters that were hiding behind the building blocks. 'Run, Scooby, run!' I called out as we played in the corner of the room. Mum sat in a chair opposite the paediatrician and speech therapist. The teaching assistant returned from her cigarette and stood in the corner of the room awkwardly, suddenly feeling out of place at being party to such an intimate moment.

I can't remember the exact wording. I want to write it here, as if it was some profound step in our journey, but it would be a lie. I can't remember if it was delivered in matter-of-fact fashion or if it was a whispered, 'I'm so sorry.' It just happened.

The Boy had autism. Mum nodded her head, slowly, taking it in. Stoic as ever, I burst into tears. I don't know why. I don't know if they were tears of relief, of sadness or of fear. Maybe the tears were my own form of biting, a release from all the anxiety. Whatever they were, they made the atmosphere a tad uncomfortable. It's all right for a mum to cry, weeping silent tears into a tissue as they talk on. But for a dad to start full-on blubbering from the corner of the room while clutching a Shaggy doll while his son screams, 'Why have you stopped playing?' is all too much.

I started to blurt out all the reasons why he couldn't be autistic, spouting every stereotype I knew. 'But he makes eye contact,' I pleaded.

'I'm sorry, John,' the paediatrician countered kindly. 'We've been in this room for nearly two and a half hours and he hasn't once looked at me, even when we had a conversation.'

'But he has an amazing imagination! We're playing "Scooby-Doo"!'

'He doesn't, John. He has *your* imagination. He copies you.'

My mind drifted away as they discussed the 'triad of impairments' with Mum, what it might mean for the future, the need to return for a chat about the genetic implications and here's some leaflets on support groups, etc. There'd be a lifetime to catch up with all that, I knew, but for now I returned to playing with The Boy, hiding my tears from him and retreating back into our world of Shaggy and Scooby-Doo. Every now and then I'd catch snippets of the conversation from the other side of the room.

'There aren't any rules. Just do what you can to get by,' the paediatrician was saying to Mum. 'You can't do any more than that.'

'It's a lifelong condition, but with the right level of support...'

Less than five minutes later and we were ready to go. All done. The Boy as oblivious to it all as he was when he walked in.

As we made for the door, the paediatrician turned to me and Mum and smiled warmly. 'You've done an amazing job,' she said. 'Your son's a wonderful boy. The only reason he's come as far as he has is because of the work you've put in. You should be very proud.'

'She says that to everyone,' I muttered as we turned up the corridor and headed for separate homes. But those parting words meant more than she would know, to both of us. After years of being told it was our fault – our parenting, our lack of boundaries, inconsistent routines – here was someone acknowledging that we'd done OK. Maybe even better than OK.

We walked past reception, seeing another family sitting, waiting. The young boy was flapping his hands constantly, rocking in his seat. Mum was scanning a leaflet, 'What to Do In The Event of a Complaint'. I almost wanted to wait, to see where their journey would take them, to see if they too were heading for the big consulting room with the mirror along one wall, taking their first precarious steps onto the conveyor belt of bad news.

Walking out into the afternoon sun, me and Mum turned to each other to say our goodbyes. 'Coffee?' she said.

'Yeah, why not?'

The Boy slipped between us and held both our hands as we set off up the road. Everything was the same, yet nothing was the same.

CHAPTER SIXTEEN

The School Run

We went shopping again the other day. Back to that super-market, the one that Dad likes because it's cheap but The Boy hates because it has people and queues and no self-service checkouts. I'd like to pretend that my decision to involve him in the shopping experience was a deliberate one because I wanted to teach him some independent life skills but, if I'm honest, I took him with me because I couldn't be arsed going while he was at school.

We were all done in approximately seven minutes. For someone with mobility difficulties, he can't half whizz around a supermarket. There was stuff in the trolley, some of it looked green: success. We got to the till, a bit of a queue but not too bad. Dad had even remembered to bring his own carrier bags in the days before it was even law. What a virtuous pair we were.

Then an old dear shuffled up behind us in the queue. She had half a dozen eggs and that was it. I thought I would set an example for my son. 'Would you like to go in front?' I said to her, stepping aside and gesturing as if I'd just offered her a damehood.

'Thank you,' she said, 'very kind.'

I smiled to myself. That warm feeling of pleasing someone. Knowing she thinks I am now a perfect father and a perfect human being. All is well.

As she stood in front of us in the line, now inches away, I didn't spot The Boy's face. I was too busy trying to work out the number of calories in a flapjack. If I had, I might have spotted the reddening and pre-empted what was about to happen.

'BIT RUDE!' he shouted at the top of his voice. Oh dear, no build-up with this one. Whatever had upset him had gone straight into the danger zone. 'YOU!' he yelled, pointing at me, 'HOW DARE YOU LET AN OLD WOMAN PUSH PAST YOUR SON. HOW RUDE! RUDE MAN! SHE WAS BEHIND US! YOU LET HER PUSH IN!!!'

Here we go. The old dear turned round, glaring. People stared. Pointed. Whispered. The Boy continued right the way through the queue and out of the shop. Ramming me with the trolley. Screaming, hitting. But finally, after years of angst and worry, I don't care as much what people think when things go awry. Maybe Mr People Pleaser has finally come to terms with his son's behaviour. Or maybe it's just that now he's a bit older it's more obvious something is different with him than when he was a toddler.

We got outside and, as always seems to happen, the calmness and quiet of the car brings him back to himself. And this might seem strange for some people to grasp, but I apologized to him. And I didn't do it just to try to placate him. I'd forgotten to see the world as he sees it. In his world I'd broken the rules. Rule No. 11,967 – filed in his head under Queuing – the rule that you never push in, I'd broken it.

I imagine this is the way life is for The Boy. In his head there is a huge filing system, compartmentalized into the different categories of Rules for Living, the only way he can make sense of the world. Things you do and things you don't do, learnt over the years with hundreds of new rules added each day. Every outburst comes when there's a variant, when the rules suddenly change. That's why routine gives him comfort. For years I tried to introduce the concept of a cooked breakfast once in a while. But he couldn't cope with that. Because breakfast is a bowl and a spoon. It isn't a plate and a knife and fork. That's dinner. And for him to be able to cope with that seemingly small change in routine meant in his head he was rewriting and then re-learning the Dinner rule, the Breakfast rule, the Cutlery rule, the Days of the Week rule and so many other rules that he'd spent years mastering and now all of a sudden they had to be re-learnt and re-cross-referenced and filed.

And now I've ruined the Queuing rule. Yes, he knows now that people can push in sometimes. But what is the rule? Did

I let her in front of us because she's old or because she has six eggs or because she was wearing a green coat? Was it because it was 4.06 p.m., because it was a Wednesday or because it was raining outside? The Boy can't be sure, so all he can do now is write a rule to cover every possibility. Until something happens to change it. And then they can all be re-written again and so this confusing life goes on and on and on.

Each time I remember to stop and see things through his eyes, it makes me appreciate him even more, to be almost in awe of him and others like him when I think of the battles that rage inside their heads daily. And to remind myself of just how far he's come. Yes, I need to help him to work on his outbursts and controlling his aggression, but it will come. And it will come by trying to understand him that little bit more each day.

So, today Dad has added Rule No. 784,678 to his own Rules for Living. To keep remembering to look at the world through the eyes of another. It's amazing what you can learn.

MY SON'S NOT RAINMAN BLOG

The emotions of the days and weeks that followed the diagnosis were strange, more variable and unpredictable than the hot water in my mum's electric shower. There was relief – relief that we finally had a reason, an explanation and, I suppose, relief that we weren't responsible. Then came guilt – guilt for making this all about us when The Boy was still none the wiser, guilt for not getting him there sooner. There was fear too – fear for the future, not knowing what progress he'd make. And googling for answers, too, endlessly trawling the Internet but never quite getting the answer I wanted which is that everything will be just fine. Overall, I suppose there was sadness. Sadness for him, sadness for all of us.

We went back the following week to meet the paediatrician once more for a chat about genetics, about the increased risk of any of our subsequent children having autism. It seemed bizarre to be sharing this conversation with the person who used to be my wife. We smiled and nodded politely throughout. There will be no siblings.

'Use the diagnosis to access services' had been the initial advice. Now we had a diagnosis, people had to sit up, to listen. However, rather than open doors it closed them, at least at first. The play therapy that had been our only real success, surely we could return to that now. 'No, I'm afraid not. Your son has autism. That's the reason for his behaviour. We can no longer offer you play therapy. There are a number of parent support groups in your area for you to chat to other people in a similar situation.'

I took down the details but never went. I didn't want to chat to other people about their children, I wanted it all to be about mine. And part of me still felt awful, still felt like we didn't belong with the autism group. Fearing that we wouldn't be accepted because we didn't have 'proper' autism. We didn't have the hand-flapping, little-boy-lost autism. We had the feisty, challenging one.

At least the diagnosis made a big difference on the school front. Turns out it's harder to continually exclude a child with an autism diagnosis – Disability Discrimination Act and all that. We were now in year one and I'd stopped going in every lunchtime. I was still called unofficially, though, if not daily then every couple of days. It's tough to know what to do as a parent – schools aren't allowed to exclude your child unless it's done formally, but they'll phone you up and tell you, 'We just want you to know he isn't having a good day.' I'd hear The Boy screaming or crying uncontrollably in the background and it used to break me. On paper I should have left him at school rather than coming to collect him, but sometimes as parents our hearts rule our heads. And I still believe that isn't necessarily a bad thing.

The school now had the evidence to apply for a statement of special educational needs. This is a formal document detailing a child's learning difficulties and the help that will be given. The idea is that if your child needs help at school – beyond what their teachers can provide – the statement will ensure they get the right help. It's only really necessary if the school is unable to meet a child's needs on its own. It's important not just for parents but for schools too – it means additional funding, and a school that is named in the statement has a legal obligation to educate that child. (At the time of writing in 2016, statements of special educational needs are being phased out in the UK and replaced with education and health-care plans.)

And so another meeting was scheduled with the head teacher. The paperwork was ready to be sent through to make the statement application. But there was a sticking point. The school felt it was the end of the line for them. 'We don't feel we have the expertise in-house. We think a specialist provision may be the best setting for him. I'm sorry, John. We're unable to meet his needs.'

How many more times over the years would I hear those words – 'unable to meet his needs'? And how many more schools would The Boy have to go through before he finally settled?

The irony was that the children who made the most noise left school with the least – mid-term, mid-week, even mid-lesson. Almost smuggled out of the back door. A few weeks later a parent might ask, 'Where's such and such?'

'Oh, he left,' would come the reply. 'It was felt the school wasn't right for him.'

I understand how incredibly difficult it could be, teaching a child who could be as disruptive as The Boy, especially while trying to meet the needs of the rest of the class. I got all that. But I had to see it from his perspective – every 'unable to meet his needs' has affected him, left him wondering why he suddenly can't see his friends anymore, not really understanding any of it. They've left a mark on him like a badly drawn tattoo. It may well fade with time, but it will always be there. And so, with the decision made, I made an appointment with Mum to visit the local special school.

I'm not sure what we were expecting when we turned up. Even if I wouldn't admit it at the time, I was scared. Scared at what I'd find. Scared that I wouldn't interact in the right way, wouldn't do the right thing. It just felt strange. Yet, walking through the door, everything seemed so ordinary. Everyone seemed so matter-of-fact about it all and it all seemed so run-of-the-mill. I found myself desperate to see the other children, to see what they looked like. I needed to grade them in my head, to see if they were 'better' or 'worse' than The Boy. What a messed-up way of looking at the world.

The head teacher met us to take us on a tour of the school. She explained that we might see some behaviours that were different and that it could be difficult for some of the children to deal with strangers coming into the classroom. For that reason we wouldn't enter every class. She spoke on one level the whole time, no rise or fall in her voice, no facial expressions whatsoever. I thought how much The Boy would like the consistency, the sameness – but how unnerving it seemed to me.

As we walked through the school I was struck by how 'school-like' it looked, how normal. That fear I had when I first walked in there was real. Even the very notion of disability was still new to me and I suppose it terrified the life out of me. There was a comfort in seeing a school hall looking like a school hall and a playground looking like a playground. It made it all feel a bit less daunting. There were even display boards filled with children's work. I scanned them, taking it all in, looking for evidence of how old the children were, who'd created the work, how severe or otherwise their disability might have been.

We entered the reception class with the youngest children in the school. It was warm and friendly – a happy place. They say a picture paints a thousand words and never was that more true than in a special school. Visuals everywhere, small cartoon drawings showing what was happening now and next, what day it was, when lunch was. There were about ten children in the room and three staff. It struck me how calm it seemed, how quiet compared to The Boy's previous mainstream class of thirty-one.

As we made our way towards the next classroom, the head stopped us in our tracks. 'There is a young boy in the next class who finds people visiting the school particularly difficult. For that reason we won't go in and disturb the lesson, but given it's the class your son might join should he come to the school, you can have a look through the window of the classroom door.'

I looked, taking everything in, planning The Boy's life in twenty seconds. If this was to be his class, I needed to see what role the people inside might play. Who would be his friend? Who would come round to play? What did the teaching assistants look like? Did the teacher look happy? A boy in the corner of the room spotted me. He grinned and, quick as a flash, he ran towards the door. As he got closer, he flung his entire body at the door, pressing his hands and face against the glass window and wailing at the top of his voice, 'HELP ME! THIS IS HELL ON EARTH!'

I swear he grinned at me again as a teaching assistant gently led him back to his seat. 'That's Aaron,' the head said, completely unfazed as she pushed open the double doors at the end of the corridor. 'Aaron sometimes has difficulty expressing himself.'

I turned to The Boy's mum and smiled. We'd found our school.

CHAPTER SEVENTEEN

Working Nine to Five

Yesterday was teacher training day, so a day off for The Boy. I decided to drag him away from the computer screen. I took him to Legoland. I grant you, it wasn't the wisest decision I've ever made in my life. Partly because the other eight million people who live in London seemed to have also decided that yesterday was the perfect opportunity to visit Legoland.

The Boy coped well with the two-hour tailback getting into the car park; he even managed the one-hour queue at 'guest services' for the exit pass to help children on the rides who can't cope with queuing (oh, the irony). We were finally in. The Land of Lego.

Legoland is great for playing Spot the Person On The Autistic Spectrum. The place is filled with them. I may well be playing to stereotypes again, but Lego seems to hold a fascination for so many autistic children. It is the brick that never changes; it is consistent from one day to the next. The brick you can build walls with to keep the confusing world outside. I spent the day happily muttering to myself, 'He's one,' or 'She's on the spectrum, her mum and dad just don't know it yet.'

We only went on a couple of rides. There's a favourite one we both like – Fairy Tale Brook. It's a really slow, gentle ride in a small boat that takes you through different fairytale scenes made out of Lego. The ride is full of new mothers, babes in arms and small toddlers oohing and aaahing their way around. And then us two lumps join them and The Boy's voice cuts through the gentle music and air of serenity as he comments at the top of his voice on what has changed since we were last there three years ago and how it's not even a real boat we're sitting in.

Rides aren't really the reason to visit Legoland though. Rides just detract from the main event, the Lego. We spent two hours in one room where you can make cars out of Lego and race other people's cars down a ramp. The Boy liked it because all the children in the room were at least half his age and, frankly, they were amateurs, wasting time building elaborate contraptions when The Boy had realized that if you want to win a Lego car race all you need is an axle and two wheels. He kicked the arse of every toddler that dared to take him on. Top dog.

Then The Boy's highlight of the day: *Star Wars* Miniland, a whole exhibition where scenes from *Star Wars* are recreated in Lego. Utopia. We spent forever in there. It was dark, so The Boy clung to me with one arm as I pushed his wheelchair with the other, but the darkness also seemed to help him be himself. As we approached each exhibit he became excited and animated as he talked through each scene in front of us, hand gestures to emphasize points, sharing knowledge I never even knew he had. It was like a light went on inside him and he was able to express himself in ways he never can usually, and even in the darkness his eyes shone with delight and wonder. And yes, it probably would have been easier to understand him if he'd taken a breath once in a while, but it was one of those all-too-rare moments where he really seemed, I don't know, connected.

Dad's highlight of the day? Apart from the drive around the M25, it was in the room where we raced the cars down the ramp. There was another lad I'd identified quite clearly as being 'one of us' some time earlier. And although he was at least half The Boy's age, the two of them seemed drawn to each other. Birds of a feather. They never spoke, but they raced side by side for quite a while. And, as we went to leave, I told The Boy to put his two wheels and axle back. The winning car. Instead, he walked over and, without saying a word, just put it on the floor next to the other boy's feet and the two of them looked at each other and smiled. A gift, for a friend.

MY SON'S NOT RAINMAN BLOG

As The Boy was due to start at his new school, I started to think about returning to work. It had been a long time and I was unsure what I wanted to do anymore. It's fair to say my work history could best be described as 'chequered'. A fifty-four-page CV listing jobs lasting little more than a few years.

The middle of the 1990s seemed to be the era of the temp contract, with employment agencies popping up left, right and centre, and the terms they offered suited me down to the ground. I won't give you the full list here, but I've been around a bit – a chicken factory at the age of eighteen and by the age of twenty-two I'd worked in warehouses, shampoo factories and even fitted the odd bit of double glazing. I moved down to London with a loan from the bank based on a trainee management position at a leading retailer (I had a temp job in their warehouse for a fortnight, but don't tell the bank that) and started a job stuffing envelopes before falling into a succession of different admin jobs in the city. I settled down a bit, eventually, finally working for a management consultant, spending half the week in Amsterdam and half in London, thinking I'd hit the big time as I flew between the two on business-class flights. I felt I was *it*, in my cheap suits, bouncing cheques at exchange booths in airports. But all of that was before The Boy, before I became ill, before any of this. Before.

I knew I didn't want to go back to those days. Something had shifted and I couldn't decide what it was. Part of me thought that having The Boy taught me a sense of responsibility, that now we were on our own it was time to grow up. But maybe it taught me the opposite. Maybe the time I spent supporting him at school, trying to encourage him to make friends, entertaining him through the darker times, maybe it taught me the value of playing, of trying to be carefree. I thought of getting a job as a teaching assistant, but I really didn't want to teach – there was certainly too much responsibility in algebra and fractions and following someone else's idea of a curriculum. 'Play' was the thing I kept coming back to – from play therapy to trying to engage with The Boy in the moments when I'd 'lost' him – it had become an incredibly important part of our lives. Play is a very under-rated thing.

A job came up in a children's care home, less than a mile up the road. It was a respite centre for children with severe disabilities, somewhere where they could come and spend a weekend or a few days every couple of months to provide a break for their parents and carers. I loved the sound of it – a place for the children to play, have fun, do whatever they wanted to do and be whoever they wanted to be without the constraints of having to follow a learning plan or strict rules.

I did more background work to prepare for that job than I have for any position before or since. I knew I wanted it. Every Child Matters, the Five Outcomes for a Child, the local authority's safeguarding policy, I knew them all. The hours were rubbish (shift work with early starts, late evenings and sleepovers across weekends) but The Boy's mum agreed to be as flexible as possible. And the pay was even worse – on a par with the shampoo factory from some years earlier. I knew our lives were different now, but it was a chance to get back to some semblance of normality. And maybe it was a chance to put everything we'd been through into some perspective.

I'm not sure what I was expecting on that first day. The other staff were wary – here was someone with no experience or real background in professional care. My first shift was spent working with a young man we'll call Joe. Joe, like The Boy, was diagnosed with autism. Yet it was there, in that one word, where the similarity ended. Joe was around fifteen years of age and towered over The Boy in every way. He had learning difficulties, was non-verbal and doubly incontinent. Joe had been given photographs of me to help him cope with the new face but it didn't seem to be enough. As I walked into the room to meet him, Joe became distressed and tried to attack me, pushing me away, hitting out.

Worse yet, he then turned his fear and anger onto himself, punching away at himself with a voracity I'd never seen. It was heart-breaking, seeing the distress I was causing and not knowing what to do about it. The other staff stepped in, comforting Joe, reassuring him that things were OK. I stepped away from him, feeling like I'd failed, and spent the rest of the shift hiding in the office reading care plans, finding safety amongst the paperwork.

I walked home at the end of my first shift feeling like I'd made the biggest mistake of my life. It seems callous writing this now, but I can think of no other way to put it – I didn't know children like Joe existed. I thought disability was hoists and wheelchairs and lullabies and I thought autism was The Boy. I didn't know it could be all those things plus fear and anger and sadness and violence. Maybe I was naive or maybe we need to educate people more about the levels of disability in this world.

I'm sorry Joe. I didn't know.

Slowly, over the days and weeks that followed, I began to build up a relationship with Joe and the other children. It became the most incredible job I've ever had. I never knew what each shift would bring. There was the young man who became so distressed at rainfall he'd try to pull fire extinguishers off the wall the moment the skies turned grey; the teenager who hated the feeling of clothes against his skin and would constantly try to rip them off; the young blind girl with a love of lip-balm and an incredible knowledge of radio station frequencies. And what struck me the most was how these children had spent their lives being dismissed as being unable to communicate, yet they imparted their needs loud and clear in their every action. Every cry and every smile – in some cases, even every blink. The irony is that they were talking to a deaf world.

It's an odd conundrum, working in care. Here was a job that felt like the most important one I'd ever held, in which I earned the least amount of money I'd ever been paid. Not since the heady days of putting the caps on 500 ml bottles of conditioner in the shampoo factory had I seen so little cash. And I still felt a bit of a fraud – would I ever have considered such a job if my own son hadn't introduced me to this world? I doubt it. Cashing cheques to ensure I had enough money to get me through the weekend was a much more attractive option.

I saw the frustrations of what being a care worker entailed: being told there wasn't enough money to take the children out on a trip then discovering boxes of expensive stationery ready to be thrown out due to 'rebranding'; jobs in jeopardy due to the tendering process; the endless paperwork and form-filling on antiquated computers that was an integral part of a job chosen by those who had shunned the office world in search of a hands-on job. It often seemed that the powers that be wanted to read about good care rather than witness it. Risk assessments, shift write-ups and care plans intruded on the care itself. People don't go into care for money, we all know that. But give them job security, make them feel valued and appreciated and it all comes full circle.

And then I saw the families and what they went through. People whose children never slept, whose behaviour made The Boy look like Mother Theresa, who came through the doors beyond tired, only to learn that they were now to only get two nappies allocated a day or that the Saturday morning playgroup was to close due to lack of funding.

I took the test to drive the minibus and that became my favourite activity. So many of the youngsters hadn't been on many trips away – lack of transport for some, 'too much of a risk' for others. Three members of staff took one twelve-year-old boy to the seaside for the first time in his life, led him down to the sea, which he decided he never wanted to leave, and it took us two and a half hours to convince him to come back to the minibus; I took a boy who loved Chelsea on a tour of the club and who was so overcome with excitement he just decided to shout 'F*CK! F*CK! F*CK! F*CK!' all the way around, much to the bemusement of the other visitors. Those trips out became as much about other people as they did about the children. My first shift with Joe had shaped my time there – as much as I wanted to allow the children to do everything they had always been deprived the chance of doing, I wanted to ensure we went out as much as possible. I wanted people to meet Joe and Adam and Sarah and John...

The Boy used to come and visit the respite centre. He loved it. There was a sensory room, a soft-play room, an IT suite and six bedrooms. We'd pop in now and then when I wasn't working, say 'Hello' to some of the young people and stop for dinner. He always wanted to stay the night, loved the idea of the bath that moved up and down when you pressed a button and always eyed with suspicion the young person who'd be staying in room three – that was the room he wanted to stay the night in. It had a television and some of the older boys would try to sneak a peek at Babestation if you didn't catch them quickly.

My favourite memory of that time was the Christmas party. All the young people were invited and the Salvation Army band came along for carols that no one wanted as it was just delaying the sausage rolls. It was a brilliant event.

I was asked to be Father Christmas. I agreed. Like most immature men of advancing years I had a costume at the ready

187

and a body that had long been in training for such a momentous occasion. There was one condition though; The Boy would have to come with me.

I sat him down and explained that Father Christmas had asked us to do him a favour. The Big Man couldn't make it to the party himself as he was so busy getting ready and wanted to know if we could help him out. I would be Father Christmas and he'd asked The Boy to be an elf. The Boy happily agreed.

At first the elf costume was, of course, too itchy and the pointy ears I purchased were never going to happen, nor the red, rosy cheeks. But after some cajoling and with 'normal' clothes underneath, the elf was sort of dressed for the occasion.

I'll be honest, I hadn't really thought the whole thing through. I imagined it would just be Santa sitting in his big chair while at his feet perched his doe-eyed elf, looking up at him with wide-eyed wonderment, passing presents to the delighted children who wandered in with their parents.

The staff had spent a week turning the sensory room into a grotto. That's what I loved about that place and they'd completely gone to town on it. The party was only scheduled to run for two hours, but here was a grotto any department store would be proud of. Once we arrived and I went to get changed into my costume in the staff sleep-in room, I was trying to remind The Boy not to call me Daddy. 'It's your name,' he said. I reminded him that I was meant to be Santa and he was meant to be an elf. He nodded, said 'I know' and then called me Daddy every time he spoke to me. I just told all the bewildered-looking children and parents who filed in that 'I was like a father' to the elves in the workshop.

And so began one of the strangest one hundred and twenty minutes of my life. The Boy loved every bit of it. Between banging presents on the floor and eating mince pies, it turned out he had quite a lot to say to the children who came to visit Santa that day. As gentle Christmas music filled the sparkling festive sanctuary, I gave a performance Sir Ian McKellen would have been proud of. And as I talked wistfully about magic dust and children sleeping soundly while the sleigh bells tinkled in the cold December night, the elf had his own script to work from.

'BE GOOD OR YOU WON'T GET ANYTHING!' he barked at them. 'WILL THEY, DADDY?'

As I asked each child what they wanted for Christmas, the elf would once again pass his opinion.

'I'VE GOT THAT.'

'YOU CAN'T WATCH THAT. IT'S GOT SWEARING IN.'

'RUBB-ISH.'

Then came the lovely photograph with Father Christmas, a memory to cherish for years to come. And, as each parent went to capture the moment, with perfect timing a wild-eyed grimacing elf would suddenly leap up to occupy the screen where their loved one was meant to be. As the child went to leave, I asked the elf to pass me a small, wrapped present for them to take away. Each time he just threw the present in the general direction of the door for them to collect on their way out.

'IT'S A SELECTION BOX. THEY'RE ALL THE SAME.'

I've done lots of jobs in my lifetime. Some crap ones, some not so crap. Yet I genuinely can't think of a single position that has even come close to teaching me as much about life and the human condition as those two years in the care home. I think I'd have stayed longer if The Boy's school days hadn't once again become unsettled. I learnt that the bravest people in the world aren't necessarily the loudest and that there's courage in the small things, in the everyday. I learnt that loving someone isn't always about walking over hot coals or making big bold statements and declarations. It can often be about doing the things you don't want to do, day after day. And I learnt that while McDonald's might not provide the most nutritious food in the land, it doesn't half come in handy when you're trying to coax someone out of the sea and into the back of a minibus.

CHAPTER EIGHTEEN

Legs Eleven

Last night all the worries and traumas of the last couple of weeks melted away. Last night... *Doctor Who* returned.

Given it was the fiftieth anniversary, it was being shown simultaneously at the cinema as well as on TV and I'd taken a gamble a few weeks ago and booked seats. 3-D. Near the back. The Boy hates 3-D. And sitting near the back. But this was the Doctor. Normal rules don't apply.

Trips out so rarely cause The Boy excitement. He will enjoy himself while he's there, but often the change in routine and accompanying anxiety means it can be a battle to get him out of the house in the first place. The neighbours must think I'm dragging him off to the orphanage by the noise and protest, rather than the family trip swimming or to the park.

But yesterday from the minute he woke up he started asking, 'How much longer?' At 5.00 p.m. he had his shoes on. By 5.30 p.m. he'd even brushed his teeth. We left the house with him leading the way, not dragging his feet at the back like usual. This was a trip like no other.

In the car, I was allowed to have the stereo on. And even the heater. The adrenaline and excitement surging through his body meant that he was suddenly able to cope with things that he couldn't normally deal with. Once he told me that he doesn't like going in a car at night because it's dark on the floor where your feet are but tonight it doesn't matter as he's going to see *Doctor Who*.

We arrived at the cinema fashionably early. We'd had to park quite far away and I suggested we use the wheelchair. He gave me a look as if to say, 'How do you expect me to save Gallifrey in a bloody wheelchair?' So we walked instead. Well, I walked. He practically skipped.

We collected our tickets. I asked him if he wanted popcorn. Once again, I got the look. There would be no food or drink. How can you eat and drink and concentrate at the same time? Fine by me. Cheap date.

Then I saw the queue. My heart sank. It had all gone so well up to this point. I warned The Boy it could be a long wait. 'Doesn't matter,' he said. For twenty minutes he queued. At one point we were stood next to a poster advertising the film itself. He turned to me, his face about to explode. 'I can't stand near that,' he said, 'I just want to touch it. It's too exciting!'

Finally, they let us through. I went to walk towards the lifts as we always do but The Boy dragged me back. 'Let's go with everyone else,' he said.

'Are you sure?' He nodded, beaming away. So last night, among a sea of bow ties, fezzes and *Doctor Who* scarves, a boy and his dad rode the escalator.

We took our seats, The Boy on the aisle with no one next to him. His 3-D glasses that he hates wearing were on ten minutes early. The theme music started and he began accompanying it. 'Woo-ooh,' he wailed.

'Shush!' I said, laughing.

'I just can't help it!' he replied.

I'm not sure what happened for the rest of the film. The Boy was lost in it all. Every now and then I'd glance over, seeing the lights from the screen dance across his face. Mesmerized. The film ended. Exhausted, The Boy slumped back in his chair, silent.

'Come on, kiddo,' I said, helping him on with his coat, 'time to go home. Let's go and get the lift.'

MY SON'S NOT RAINMAN BLOG

The diagnosis of autism helped in other areas as well as with the school. We still had so many concerns regarding The Boy's legs. We'd managed to get a physiotherapy referral but 'tight hamstrings' was the furthest we'd got up to this point. Yet having the word 'autism' attached to medical records seemed to make people listen far more than they ever had previously. Maybe it was all just a coincidence, but less than six months after that first diagnosis the three of us found ourselves at King's College, London to see a neurologist.

'Hellooo, I'm Michael!' he beamed, with a demeanour more suited to a children's television presenter than the senior hospital consultant he was. I liked him instantly, as did The Boy. 'Now then, young man, let's take a little look at you. I normally ask people who come to see me to walk up and down the corridor outside for me, but I bet you can't do that...'

The Boy did exactly as Michael asked. Some people just have a natural way with children, whatever diagnosis or condition they may present with. Despite the numerous autism strategies and guidelines, sometimes there's just something inbuilt, something inherent in a person that can't be taught, something that enables them to communicate across all levels. Whatever that magic 'thing' is, Michael had it in spades.

'Wow! You are brilliant at that! I bet you can't do that again for me?' he said, as The Boy turned to strut his stuff up and down the hospital catwalk once more, keen to please his new friend.

'Super stuff! Now, let's do the boring bit and have a closer look at those legs. Do you like *Ben 10*? Ah, *Power Rangers*, eh? I think Dad would look quite fetching in one of their outfits.'

Eventually, the poking and prodding was over. The Boy, having been to enough appointments to know the drill by now, knew it was his turn to chill out. It seemed that in every consulting room across the land there sits a magic cupboard in the corner of the room with a few stark wooden toys inside – just enough to crash and bang through the boring talking bit.

'Well,' said Michael, that reassuring smile never quite leaving his face, 'I'm 99.5 per cent certain it's cerebral palsy. It looks like spastic diplegia. The tightness in the muscles, the walking gait, they all point to that. It's mild, if that's the case. We'll need a CAT scan of the brain, just to be sure.'

I don't remember what I thought driving home. I didn't think too much about things really – I think that word 'mild' had given us some reassurance. Spastic diplegia. I promised myself that whatever I did I wouldn't look online; there was nothing to be gained from that. There was a queue getting out of the hospital car park. By the time we'd reached the barrier I was on page two of Google hits. There were even videos of children with the same condition on YouTube. The way they walked, the position of their legs, they were just like The Boy.

Rather than being comforted by them, the clips sent my mind into a tailspin. How had it been missed all these years? It all seemed so obvious suddenly. And that word, 'spastic'. I was a child of the 1970s, the era of the Spastic Society, and even now the ignorant associations of that word echoed round my head as the insults had across countless school playgrounds all those years ago.

The CAT scan some weeks later confirmed things. Cerebral palsy.

Cerebral palsy is a condition that affects muscle control and movement. It's usually caused by an injury to the brain before, during or after birth. Children with cerebral palsy have difficulties in controlling muscles and movements as they grow and develop. There may be no obvious single reason why a child has cerebral palsy. The main causes of cerebral palsy include:

- Infection in the early part of pregnancy
- Lack of oxygen to the brain
- Abnormal brain development
- Genetic link

Present in around 75–88 per cent of people with cerebral palsy, spasticity means the muscle tone is tight and stiff, causing a decreased range of movement. As the muscle tone is so tight, spasticity can be very painful with muscles often going into spasm. It can affect many different areas of the body.

SCOPE.ORG.UK

'The condition isn't in itself degenerative,' Michael reassured us on our next visit, still smiling away. 'However, as the child grows it will become harder for the leg muscles to support the body. We'll do some physiotherapy to try to maintain strength and there are some surgical options we can look at down the line. I've made a referral to the wheelchair service for you. They'll be in touch.'

And that was the first time that word was used, 'wheelchair'. This was a boy who had been diagnosed with knock-knees and suddenly here we were discussing wheelchairs. 'It will help with longer distances,' said Michael, 'just to walk and keep up with his peers. He's expending around ten times the energy of his friends. Use a wheelchair to prevent tiredness. He's a child – keep that energy for the playground when you get there, not for the walk to the playground.'

A wheelchair. But I could carry him on my shoulders. That's what we'd always done. And besides, I thought this was *mild*? Mild means a couple of ibuprofen and a lie-down in a darkened room for a few hours. Mild means not quite feeling yourself for a few days. It doesn't mean wheelchairs and mobility issues for the rest of your life. That's not mild.

Over the weeks that followed, my anger seemed to grow inside me. Anger that The Boy had had to wait so long for a diagnosis; anger that, as parents, we once again hadn't pushed enough; anger at myself for the number of times I didn't listen when The Boy refused to move any more, not realizing that it was never defiance but pain that stopped him in his tracks. I played back the previous paediatrician's appointment and the advice to 'sort his behaviour out first'. The ugly reality of his so-called 'behaviour issues' was that they prevented getting the very answers that might have curbed those same behaviours in the first place. An earlier diagnosis wouldn't have cured him, I'm not naive enough to suggest that. But it might have helped with his discomfort and his pain.

Why didn't I push enough? The self-flagellation may be wearing a little thin now, but it's something I've felt guilty about throughout The Boy's life. Schools that were failing him, health-care professionals who didn't listen, support that was promised but never given – I should have pushed more. As parents we really can't win sometimes – if we push and push for everything then we are seen as 'very difficult' and services are withheld as a result; if we don't push enough then we don't get the services our children deserve. It's a shitty game with no winners.

For the most part, it was never a doctor or teacher or physiotherapist I really wanted to see. I think it was a clairvoyant. I was only too aware of how his conditions were affecting him day-to-day; we lived through those experiences each and every moment, alongside him. But I wanted to know how they would affect him next week, next month, next year. I presumed that university was off the cards now, but what about GCSEs? Would he marry the girl of his dreams? Come on Dr Michael, crack out your crystal ball, give me the answers to the big questions.

'I can't predict the future,' Michael said after a long pause at a follow-up appointment some months later. 'At this stage it's difficult to say. As he grows, he will become more reliant on his wheelchair. I envisage that into adulthood he'll be able to get around indoors, inside a flat or house, without too much difficulty. However, he'll probably be reliant on a wheelchair for travel outside. As I say, it's very difficult to predict.'

We said nothing, just nodding back at the kind, smiling face sitting across the consulting room. In the corner a small boy banged away at the wooden toys he was playing with, once again oblivious to it all.

'Is there anything else you'd like to know?' Michael asked, wrapping things up.

Me and Mum turned to each other. 'No, we think that's everything,' came the reply.

How my lips lied that day. Inside my head a voice was screaming, but the words just wouldn't come out. 'Actually, there is one more thing. Look closer into your crystal ball, Dr Michael. Please, one more time, before the light fades. I know you're running late with your clinic, but it's an important question, maybe the biggest one of all. This young man you see, when you look into the future, this adult who is living in the house you mentioned earlier... is he happy, Dr Michael? Is he?'

CHAPTER NINETEEN

Disco Fever

Sometimes it takes an anniversary of doing something you've done for years to remember just how far The Boy has come. This week that reminder came in the form of the Christmas tree.

The tree used to be such an upheaval for him. And you can't blame him really. Things were going quite nicely in his world; he knew where he was with everything and then, once a year, Dad would insist on moving the furniture round and sticking a seven-foot plastic tree with flashing lights in the middle of the lounge where the TV should be. Little wonder it was pulled down every other day.

But now we've become accustomed to it. The tree has become part of our routine like everything else. The same tree, with the same decorations, in the same place. Granted, if Dad had known the tree was meant to last ten years he might have selected a specimen other than the cheap supermarket one he got at the time, but it's our tree all the same.

The Boy doesn't help with decorating the tree. Boring. I learnt my lesson last year when I insisted he help and he lined up all the same size baubles of the same colour on the same branch. Instead, he turns up now for the big switch-on. Much like London's Regent Street had the Spice Girls to turn on their lights, in 2013 we once again had The Boy in his pants to do ours.

We even have a fairy nowadays too, sitting atop and surveying the chaos below. For two years she was left abandoned in the cupboard and replaced with a sellotaped-on Power Ranger. I reminded him of it the other day and I could see on his face that look of, Let's do that again! But he let it go.

The tree is in the lounge, which has recently been christened 'Dad's Room'. The Boy's bedroom next door is now apparently 'My Room'. Given he spends so much time in there, I asked if he'd like to get some Christmas decorations for 'My Room' too. To my surprise, he said yes. So off we went to the Pound Shop.

The Pound Shop is perfect for us, not least because it's a pound shop. The Boy still hasn't fully grasped the concept of money and, although he is getting better at it, he still thinks purely in terms of 'How many things can I have?' And the Pound Shop is the only place where I can be sure I'm giving the right answer without bankrupting myself. Ten things. Ten things to decorate your room for Christmas.

You can imagine how tasteful the bedroom looks now. Resplendent in its glory. It has been decorated with the subtlety of a Royal British Legion social club function room. And in the middle of it, on his chest of drawers, sits the elixir of life, the very reason to get up in the morning – his chocolate advent calendar. Breakfast.

Oh, and for designers of chocolate advent calendars, I've got a message for you. The Boy tells me he could do your job better than all of you. You can't even put the numbers one to twenty-four in the right order.

MY SON'S NOT RAINMAN BLOG

I t had been an eventful year, there was no question about that. And, as it neared its end, I had little idea that the biggest occasion was yet to come, but this time for all the right reasons. My time working in the care home, The Boy settling into his special school, the two seemed to coincide. Christmas is often described as being a 'magical time', but I'm not sure of that. I do believe though that there's something in the air at Christmas; maybe the reminder of the wonderful times that I had with my dad at this time of year. The more I age, the more I think that Christmas isn't in itself magical; what's magical is the state of mind it sometimes puts us in, ready to open our hearts to the magic that exists all year round already. (I sound like I've been drinking. I haven't, honestly.)

I suppose I get all melancholic as December approaches because Christmas will forever be that little boy standing on the stairs waiting for the magic to happen. And on that particular Christmas, after all the ups and downs, the magic came in the shape and form of The Boy's special-school disco.

As I've already mentioned, going into school for plays/parents' evenings/bloody-anything-really had for so long been the cause of real trepidation. It took some getting used to: other parents giving us a smile as we sat next to them in the hall, rather than giving us the cold shoulder because we were the parents of 'that boy'. How little they knew him.

My first introduction to special-school events was the school play, the nativity. I'd been to school plays before, when The Boy was in mainstream. 'Inclusive education,' they called it. People often ask if I'm a fan of inclusive education and, like most things, I'm sure when it's done well it's a brilliant thing. But doing it well requires patience, training and, of course, money. Too often one or all three things from that list are missing. And, when that happens, school just becomes survival of the fittest. I met a head teacher of a special school the other day and he described the place as 'the home for the victims of inclusion... we're just here to pick up the pieces when it all goes wrong,' he said. That's not to say inclusion isn't right for some children because it certainly can be. Maybe that's the better question we should ask – does a one-size-fits-all education system really help anyone?

At The Boy's mainstream primary school, the concept of inclusiveness seemed sadly lost much of the time, stuffed down the back of the sofa only to be replaced by a huge sign reading 'Token gesture' with 'At least they're taking part' popping up from behind the armrest occasionally.

On the day of The Boy's first school play in reception class, their idea of inclusiveness was for all the 'children with additional needs' to herald a scene number. (The children weren't even designated as special needs at that point. The word 'special' comes later, with a diagnosis in hand.) That was it. The other children got to dress up, dream a little and beam away to their parents filming them on the iPad for it never to be watched again. The Boy and his ilk were numbers to be walked across the front of the stage. The Boy was 'Scene no. 3' and at the end of scene two came his big moment. As the rest of his class got into position for their song, the classroom door next to the stage opened and The Boy, with a large number 3 stapled to the front of his T-shirt, was escorted across the front of the stage by a teaching assistant. Dragged from that door to another at the opposite side of the stage, seemingly to disappear forever. Inclusion at its best.

My favourite part of that whole play was the character of 'Scene no. 4', even if he never actually appeared on stage at all. As an audience we'd already had three stage numbers by now, we knew the drill. As the song at the end of the preceding scene petered out, all eyes were fixed on the classroom door at the side of the stage, eagerly awaiting the arrival of no. 4. But no. 4 never came. Instead that classroom door swung open and you could just make out the arm of a desperate teaching assistant

beckoning no. 4 to come forward. And all you could hear echoing around the walls of the school hall was an out-of-sight
table being shoved across the classroom followed by a five-
year-old yelling at the top of his voice, 'I'M NOT F*CKING
DOING IT!'

As other parents tutted their disgust, congratulating themselves
on their decision not to invite no. 4 to their beloved's birthday
party, and the murmurs of disapproval spread round the school
hall, I found myself admiring this young boy more and more.
His ability to be true to himself, to express what he really wanted.
Even now, years later, he's the one person I remember from that
entire performance – the young boy who had the ability to stamp
his individuality on this world. Good for you, mate.

But that was all a lifetime ago. Here we were now, in the
special school and their play couldn't have been more different. There's something about special-school performances and
special schools in general – much like the young boy who was
Scene no. 4, there's an honesty to them. It's something I've learnt
to love and admire over the years – I'm an innate people pleaser
and having the ability to do something purely for yourself, for
no other reason than you've decided you want to do it, feels
refreshing. For years I thought it was the wheelchair-adapted,
light-blue minibuses with their Sunshine Variety charity logo
that marked out special schools, customarily sporting a large
scrape down one side where a teaching assistant has misjudged
the width restriction on the way to the swimming pool. But it
isn't that at all. It's their honesty.

The crippling desire to want to keep everyone happy has been the bane of my life for so long. It's only now in my forties that I realize how much it's held me back. Many years ago, when I started working as a stand-up comedian, I got my first review. It was pretty scathing – not least the line, 'He's a comic who doesn't want to risk having a viewpoint of his own.' That wasn't my comedy he was describing, it was my life.

As we filed into the hall for the play that day, the lingering smells of the school lunch were still hanging around. To all intents and purposes it started off like any other school nativity play. Maybe the finish on the set design wasn't quite to the usual standard, but it wobbled and leant precariously over the proceedings just as it should. After ten minutes the music teacher (now theatrical director and playwright) dimmed the house lights (turned off the fluorescent strip lights apart from the ones at the front of the hall), signalled to the orchestra to start up the opening bars (pressed play on the CD player) and we were off.

There is a short pause. The play opens with the two lead characters entering from the classroom door at the side of the stage. Mary and Joseph, the stars of the show. They're refusing to hold hands – in fact, Mary is striding out in front. It would be a stretch of the imagination to describe the two of them as a 'loving couple'. They are treating each other with the indifference of a husband and wife who have been married for twenty-five years. Every now and then they glance towards each other, seemingly hating the very sight. They take their seats at the front of the stage. Then there's another pause. You get used to the pauses in a special-school play. There are more pauses that afternoon than Harold Pinter used in his entire career. A pause as someone makes the last-minute decision of whether they really do want to do this or not. I love it – each pause creating tension, another reminder of lives being lived in the moment, in the here and now.

And so, after a fair old wait, during which Mary and Joseph manage to sit simultaneously together but with their backs to each other, the Three Wise Men appear. Except there's only two of them. A huge part of me wanted the third one to have his moment, to fling open the door at the side of the stage and, with his mum's tea towel wrapped round his head, once more scream the immortal words, 'I'M NOT F*CKING DOING IT!'

Alas, his is a silent protest on this occasion. Instead, the Two Wise Men join Mary and Joseph on the stage. One of them spots the sea of smartphones and iPads filming the event, grins and waves to his adoring public.

And that is pretty much it for the leading players. Everyone else in the school is a sheep, all sixty-seven of them, sitting at the side of the stage. For reasons unknown, there are no shepherds. Just half a hall of children dressed as sheep. Except one. In the middle of the homemade sheep outfits one boy sits wearing a Spiderman onesie – it's never referenced at any point. Every fourth or fifth sheep is a strategically placed teaching assistant, crouching down, arms and legs splayed, trying to pin down as many wandering sheep as possible.

Among them sits The Boy. Not on the sidelines but right in the thick of it all. He's dressed like all the others, but is easy to spot. He's wearing his sheep mask on top of his head, he isn't joining in with any of the songs and in many ways he seems completely oblivious to everything going on around him; he's just waving away to the stupid man who looks a lot like him and is giving him the thumbs-up and crying his eyes out in the third row.

I can't tell you what it meant to be in the audience that day. It wasn't a long play at all: there were a few songs and one of the sheep did a solo. Earlier that week The Boy had received his first-ever birthday-party invite and now, here he was, sitting among a group of children. My son was a sheep. Belonging. Not tagged on the end as an afterthought, but a smack-bang-in-the-middle-of-it-all sheep.

Two days later, the elation slipped, if only for a while.

It was a Thursday, a dark and overcast day that seemed to match The Boy's mood perfectly when he stepped off the school bus. I knew things weren't right with him even before he arrived home. When your child doesn't speak to you about their school day, you learn to look for other signs about how the day has gone. One sure giveaway was if The Boy was sitting next to someone on the bus that brought him home. If he was, then invariably it had been a good day; it meant he was happy and could tolerate other people around him. If he was sitting alone, it meant the day hadn't gone well. It had all become too much for him. The closer to the front of the bus he was, the worse the day had been.

That day he arrived sitting in the front seat. He stepped off the bus and burst into the flat. 'I'm not going to school tomorrow.'

'Why not, mate, it's the disco tomorrow, you've been looking forward to it for ages!'

'Not going, not going, not going, NOT GOING!!!!'

The Boy struggled that night. He couldn't settle, was aggressive, he just kept hitting out at the world. These were the moments I hated the most – you could see the fear in him, could sense the absolute terror he sometimes experienced, but could never, ever put into words.

'Come on, mate, find a way. Tell me what's wrong. Tell me.'

It got to about three in the morning and The Boy was still going strong. This fear inside him, building and building. Eventually, in the stillness of night with all the lights off and in the safety of Dad's bed, he came out with it.

'I don't want to go to school tomorrow because The Boy With No Ear is coming to school tomorrow.'

I'll let that sentence hang there for a moment.

It transpired that there was to be a boy visiting the school the next day with a view to joining in January, who looked *physically different* to the other children. So, the teachers decided to prepare the class in advance. However, the plan had backfired. The Boy had decided he didn't want to go to school with The Boy With No Ear as 'people should have ears'.

The next morning I managed to coerce The Boy onto the school bus with the lure of the disco at the end of the day and the promise that I would be there for it. Then I debated as to whether I should telephone the school to warn them that The Boy wasn't quite himself.

You see, that was the danger with schools. This whole 'fight' for education had become just that – a war. History told me that if I telephoned the school to forewarn them that The Boy 'might have an unsettled day', rather than working together, he would invariably have an unsettled day. If I said nothing, we might just get away with it. It's sad, looking back, that it had gone that way, but The Boy so often seemed to be a chameleon when it came to his emotions and his behaviour – if people expected the worst of him, that was exactly what he delivered. If people expected him to thrive and be happy…

And besides, I couldn't phone the school as I didn't know the name of the other lad involved and I really didn't want to start a conversation with 'He's a bit scared of The Boy With No Ear coming to school'. I left it and instead sat at home, mobile phone in hand, just waiting for it to ring. And, for once, it didn't ring.

At the end of school I went along as agreed to meet The Boy for the school disco, almost dreading what I would find. I can't tell you how many events, trips and activities The Boy has been excluded from over the years. Until we were in the hall for the disco I wasn't quite sure it would actually happen. However, I stood outside the classroom door and the signs were good – he was still in there. So often when I went to collect him he was in another room to 'calm down' or 'chill out' or whatever the preferred term of the day was. But today, there he was, in the classroom. By the door stood a new parent I'd never seen before. Anxious, not making eye contact, this was all new to her. Ah, I thought, she must be the mum of The Boy With No Ear. I'd like to tell you I offered a reassuring word, went over and introduced myself and put her at ease. But I didn't. The old awkwardness and shyness was never more prevalent than when standing in the school playground at home time.

Suddenly the classroom door was flung open and first out was The Boy, a big grin across his face.

'Daddy, Daddy!' he shouted. 'He's really nice, The Boy With No Ear! And he does have an ear! It's just little and in the wrong place.'

I smiled meekly at the mum stood next to me but she didn't look up from her mobile phone and so I led The Boy off towards the school hall. Disco fever.

I hadn't really known what to expect. The Boy was now eight years old and he'd never been invited to a school disco. My only knowledge of such things came from my memories of school discos thirty years ago, where the boys stood on one side of the hall and the girls stood on another, and no amount of fizzy Panda Pop could take away the awkwardness I felt, even with the new corduroy trousers from Marks & Spencer and the slim, leather piano-tie swishing from my neck.

There was no dress code for this disco. Get with the times Dad, it's the twenty-first century, wear what you want. The only dress code that seemed to be in existence that day was a gravy stain down the front of a white polo shirt from the Christmas lunch.

(Why do children wear white polo shirts? How do you clean them? There were times The Boy came home from school and his polo shirt was so dirty that I thought the dinner ladies must just line the children up against the far wall of the hall, ask them to open their mouths and then fire their lunch at them from twenty-five feet away with a spatula. I read that Justin Bieber wears his underpants just once and throws them out. Well, he might think that he's living the rock 'n' roll lifestyle but I've had white supermarket polo shirts with a lifespan shorter than Justin Bieber's pants.)

I'm not sure exactly what I was expecting as I walked into the school hall that day. All I knew as an adult was if someone had offered me a disco in the middle of the afternoon I'd be knocking down Wetherspoons' door at 9.00 a.m. and lining up Jägerbombs just to cope with the sheer, bloody misery of it all.

But a special-school disco was just *different*. Whatever was in the hall that day, I wish it could have been bottled, its essence captured in some way and spread across the globe. What a better world it would be if every single person on this planet could experience the joy and the magic of that day.

It's difficult to capture it all, to do it justice, but I'll do my best.

The DJ was a lad from the sixth form with ADHD, so each song he played lasted about twenty seconds. There were teaching assistants dancing away to 'I Will Survive' like they were at Secrets nightclub in Newcastle on a Friday night thinking nobody in the world was watching them. There was one boy contentedly hanging off the gym bars on the wall. Another boy legged it around and around in circles for no reason whatsoever other than that was entirely what he wanted to do at that precise point in his life. At the buffet, lovingly prepared by the parent–teacher association at the other end of the hall, there was one child standing mesmerized, counting the hundreds and thousands on top of the cupcakes. Another child walked past and just picked up a sausage roll, smelt it, licked it, and put it back on the pile. The freedom of that simple gesture has never left me to this day. Smell it, lick it, don't want it, put it back, pick another, who bloody-well-cares? IT DOESN'T MATTER. And at the other end of the buffet table stood a boy who was just slamming BBQ-flavoured Hula Hoops one at a time into his forehead. In the middle of all this chaos and carnage, there sat a young, blind girl in the centre of the dancefloor. And she was so lost in the music, it was almost like she'd become the beat.

Every now and then The Boy would zoom into shot. It was like watching a child come alive that day. He flung himself around that school hall as if there was no tomorrow, as if his very life depended on it.

I suppose that day was the point when I first saw him as his own person. Away from me or his mum. So often I'd questioned whether special school was right for him, and many times I'd bemoaned our lot in the world. That day I realized that he'd be OK. Like the other children, he was so at ease with himself that afternoon, just existing in the here and now. He danced as well – oh, how he danced. The thing that had been holding him back until that point wasn't the physical aspect of his cerebral

palsy, it was having the freedom to express himself, to just be…
It was magical.

I can't tell you the impact that day had on our lives. Well, my
life. It seems crazy that something as simple as a bit of music
in a hall with a few flashing lights and some defrosted frozen
food could have had a profound and lasting effect on my life.
Yet it did.

I learnt far more over the two hours of a school disco from
the so-called 'more vulnerable' members of our society than I
have from any book, professor or any of the rest of it. Would
the boy with the leather piano tie from all those years ago have
joined in that day? Not a chance. He would have been too busy
worrying what everyone else thought of him. But The Boy and
his friends… they were living in the moment. Just simply living
their lives with an intensity, a joy, a freedom and an honesty
that puts the rest of us to shame. I realized then that the real
joy in life doesn't come from the big things. At the very start
of the book I mentioned that it comes from the little moments,
the moments where we're *just being*. And as a society, we don't
celebrate *just being* enough.

And I suppose if I had one wish on that wet December
afternoon, just one wish, it was that I'd had the bottle to get up
there with them and dance the day away.

CHAPTER TWENTY

He's Behind You

Recently The Boy has become more tired, frequently taking naps at school, and his walking gait has deteriorated.

So, after speaking with his teacher, the day has come. Tomorrow The Boy takes his wheelchair to school for the first time in his life. And, although it's a day I knew was always on the horizon, maybe I thought it would be a few years away from now. The reality of it has hit home and I suppose it's knocked me a bit. It's just another reminder of how the future creeps up on us when we least expect it and with it comes that fear of what else it might bring.

I remember the first visit with The Boy to the wheelchair clinic. I hated it. It was just a feeling of unbearable sadness. All right, he had a strange walk, but we got by. Yes, he became tired on long journeys. But that's what piggybacks and fireman's lifts were for. We didn't need wheelchairs. They were for other people.

Sometimes, though, we impose our own fears and apprehensions on our children. The moment we walked into the wheelchair clinic, The Boy LOVED it. To him it was like the best bike shop in the world. Choosing between a Grifter or a BMX. Aluminium frames, puncture-proof tyres, test drives and a technician to show him how to do a spin. He's never been able to ride a bike, apart from a three-wheeler – his wheelchair was the next best thing. And what little boy wouldn't want to take their bike to school?

So he's excited about tomorrow. He can't wait to show his wheelchair off to the other kids. He has given me the instructions for the other children – they can push him, but not without asking first. He has been practising his spins (push one wheel forward, pull the other back, in case you were wondering) and is ready for the attention and glory. I have no doubt that he will be reclining in his seat as he is pushed around the playground waving to the admiring crowds from his very own Popemobile.

Last week, when The Boy was having a meltdown, the deputy head told me that for a boy with cerebral palsy, he can't half run when he doesn't want to get caught. And I'm not suggesting for one minute that he carries on doing that, but...

Run like the wind my beautiful boy, run like the wind.

MY SON'S NOT RAINMAN BLOG

In the days that followed the school disco, I tried to recreate its sights and sounds. I'd nonchalantly play the dance hit of the day, 'Tubthumping', on the stereo in the hope The Boy might recreate one of his moves, but it never happened. I'd flick the light switch on and off a few times in the lounge thinking he might throw in a moonwalk. Nothing. As with so many of the best memories in life, the moment had gone, a reminder that it was just that – a moment.

I knew I had to try to change my perspective. I had to try to find the joy that I witnessed that day. The dining room table had, over time, been piled high with paperwork relating to The Boy. It wasn't intentional, just a volume of reports – educational psychologist reports, speech and language therapist reports, physiotherapy reports, consultant reports, occupational therapy reports, statement of special educational needs, the list went on. It seemed they always needed to be referenced by someone or other, so I told myself it wasn't my inherent laziness that meant they were never filed away, it just became easier to have them all to hand.

Over the days and weeks that followed the disco, I started re-reading the reports. I'm not entirely sure what I was looking for – maybe I thought I was a detective searching for the crucial bit of evidence that had been missed that might help solve the case. Or maybe I was just looking for the positive, desperately searching for the little boy from the disco whose smile lit up the room like a mirror ball.

He wasn't there.

'Poor gross motor skills', 'lack of empathy', 'poor fine motor skills', 'trunk weakness', 'limited eye contact', 'abnormal gait', 'challenging behaviours', 'sensory difficulties', 'lack of coordination', 'intoeing', 'low verbal reasoning', 'little confidence'... blah, blah, blah... It read like a never-ending charge sheet of so-called misdemeanours from the Normal Police. Page after page listing everything The Boy *couldn't* do. And here they were, piled up on the dining table in the centre of our home, in the centre of our lives. I'd let that become us. The reports were necessary and important, I understood that. They'd helped me to understand The Boy and they'd got us access to support and help we wouldn't otherwise have had. But they'd been dominant for far too long. They didn't capture him, the very essence of him. All that vibrant strength and joy at just being in the world, it could never be found here amongst the photocopied pages from professionals with their electronic signatures and letters after their names.

I bought a filing cabinet and slowly started filing everything away. (I didn't really; I emptied one large kitchen cupboard of all the plastic food containers with their mismatched lids that never fitted properly and stuffed all the paperwork in there, but 'filing cabinet' sounds far more purposeful.) It wasn't about hiding away his diagnoses and difficulties; it was about accepting them and then moving on.

One evening I dug out old photo albums and went through folders on the computer of backed-up images from long-forgotten mobile phones. It turned out that The Boy from the school disco had been with me all along – I'd just forgotten how to look for him.

That smile as a baby. Those dimples. Sitting in the sand with socks on. Grinning away, face covered in bright-blue bubble-gum ice cream. Waving from the truck ride, head rolled back, laughing on the miniature railway. On a boat, hair blowing in the wind. In the lounge at home, playing with the marble tower. Trying to blow out the candles on a birthday cake but not quite managing it and the saliva putting the flame out instead. Wrapped tightly in a towel after a bath, with wrinkled fingers and toes. Feeding the llamas that everyone else was scared of. Chasing a chicken and catching it. Days of perfect blue.

I know this all seems kind of sickly sweet now. I'm not suggesting for one moment that life was suddenly a bed of roses because I'd discovered some half-forgotten photographs. But there was a realization that I had far more control on the outcome of all this than I'd thought up to that point. As parents, we make the weather for our children. We make the weather. And if I had failed to find the joy in any of it, how on earth could I ever expect The Boy to?

We went away on holiday a few weeks later. Not for us the searing heat of the Mediterranean, or the wild animals of Kenya. We contemplated a city break to Barcelona to drink in the sights but instead opted for a caravan park in Hastings, on the south coast of England. In March.

It was a perfect holiday in every way. Swimming in the pool, playing in the arcades and going to the clubhouse at night for cheesy entertainment and two packets of crisps for a pound. We sat through the show for as long as the crisps lasted before heading off to find something else to do. And then one night The Boy discovered his favourite game of all. Bingo.

My son likes bingo. I can feel the warm, satisfied glow of my own dad looking down from above as I write that sentence. I always felt closer to my own dad when me and The Boy went on our trips to the caravan park and I'm not sure why; it's not like they were places we ever visited as a child. Maybe it was the old gas fire in the caravan lounge and the dated furnishings that reminded me of him. Or maybe it was the role reversal, that I was the one drinking the pint and someone else had the coke. Or maybe it was just that he was a family man at heart and here family seemed to mean more than anything.

We won at bingo. Not the main prize – we got four corners (there's a name for it, I'm sure, but we were mere newcomers to the sport at this point). We won a teddy bear. The Boy even went up himself to collect it. The bingo caller popped a microphone with a big red cover under his nose. I thought The Boy was going to eat it.

'Where do you live?' he asked.

'Earth,' The Boy replied, not even looking at him, before snatching the teddy bear out of his hands and running back to the safety of his crisps.

Another night there was a character meet-and-greet where we said 'Hello' to Tom and Jerry 'for real life'. It was here I realized just how much The Boy struggled with the concept of reality and make-believe. I've seen people become star-struck when they meet their heroes, be it One Direction or Ed Sheeran. For The Boy, it was two people dressed in cat and mouse costumes. He couldn't speak, he went bright red, they held out their hands for him to shake but he just flung himself at them, arms wrapped around them, clutching them tight. For real life.

The wheelchair was never far away that holiday and that was OK too. I realized how much The Boy had struggled without it and how much it helped him to remain calm when the world got too much. I mastered the art of one-handed pushing, so the chair was alongside me rather than in front. That way we could chat away as normal.

It was funny, seeing people's reactions to the wheelchair. We'd spent most of The Boy's life to date being the subject of judgemental stares and disapproving looks at the 'naughty boy'. Yet suddenly, when that exact same boy sat in a wheelchair, he was treated with nothing but doe-eyed sympathy and concern.

On the last day of our holiday we went to play crazy golf on the seafront (one of Hastings' premier attractions). I'd parked the car quite far away and we used the wheelchair to get along to the course. There was a woman in a hut next to the golf course who took the money and I spotted her face change the minute she set eyes on the wheelchair; a small smile spread across her face, filled with warmth and compassion.

I always get such mixed emotions when the wheelchair provokes that reaction. I can't help wondering what the response might have been if we'd come along twelve months earlier without it and instead The Boy had been screaming and hitting out from tiredness and an inability to stand in line in a queue. Would he have been afforded the same warmth and compassion? Or would he have dealt with the usual judgemental glares and tutting? Whatever the truth of it, there was no doubt the wheelchair made trips out easier for both of us.

That day the lovely lady in the hut refused to take any money off us (ah, it has its upsides now and again, all this) and we made our way to the first hole. The Boy, never one for exerting himself when it isn't strictly necessary, was still sitting patiently in his wheelchair, his golf club poking up between his legs.

As we got to the hole there was a family of five in front, with the father about to tee off. He glanced up and spotted the wheelchair. He immediately stopped lining up his shot.

'Oh, please, go in front, please,' he said, moving his whole family to one side.

'No, don't worry,' I said, 'it's fine. We'll wait our turn.'

'No, no, no, no, no,' he pleaded. By this point I was thinking he might throw himself down on the ground as some form of human sacrifice. 'Please,' he continued, 'go in front, please.'

I hesitated. Largely because, dear reader, much like you, I knew what was coming. By this point the woman in the hut was leaning out to watch what was happening. There was now even a small crowd gathered along the promenade – all keen to see how exactly The Boy in the wheelchair was going to do this. We had little option but to smile gracefully and I wheeled The Boy up to the tee-off line.

The minute we were there, he put the brakes on his wheelchair and *leapt* out of it. He even gave his legs a little shake from having been sitting for so long. Then, oblivious to the stares around him, he lined up his shot. The club struck the ball.

'Yesss!' he called out. 'Hole in one!' as his putt sank perfectly into the hole.

And if that was the end of the story, that would have been almost OK. But then… then The Boy ran the twenty metres to the hole. Removed the flag, bent down, collected his ball, placed the flag back and then dashed back. Sat back in his wheelchair and took the brakes off again.

At least when the guy in *Little Britain* did something similar he had the decency to do it behind his carer's back. Because all that was left for me to do was to smile to the watching crowd and bemused family and push The Boy onwards to hole number two.

'Thank you very much!' I called out over my shoulder as we brazenly headed off, waving with one hand above my head.

'T-H-A-N-K-Y-O-O-O-U-U-U-U-U!'

CHAPTER TWENTY-ONE

School's Out for Summer

We've been out for the day. In the rain. We've been for a trip into central London or the *Doctor Who* Studios, as The Boy seems to know it.

We went past the Houses of Parliament. I tried to explain to him that it was the centre of government. No, it wasn't. It was where the Slitheen spaceship hit in episode four of the first series. Oh, yes, of course it was.

I tried to educate him, honestly I did. 'OK, then, do you know why it's called Big Ben?' I asked.

'Easy. Because it's big and it's called Ben. Stupid.'

Ah, sod it, let's do what everyone does when they come to visit one of the most famous cities in the world. Let's go to the arcades.

The Boy loves the arcades. In particular, the 2p Pusher-

Machine-Things. I don't know what their proper name is, but you put 2p in and try to win... 2p. That makes perfect sense to him.

Now anyone else would just walk into the arcade and start playing. Not us. On entering, The Boy will case the joint. He will walk around the entire arcade five or six times to select the 2p Pusher-Machine-Thing of choice. Circling. Studying. There's a science behind it that I don't know and that he won't tell me. This entire exercise must be done in silence. Eventually, he will home in on one machine. Now, that machine could have upwards of thirty slots to choose from. Each one needs to be studied. The circling continues around this one machine. The lie of the two-pence pieces is examined closely. He'll pause, as if to select a slot, only to move on again. He needs to find the exact pile of coins that his coin will land on and cause the rest to become dislodged and fall down the chute. This whole process takes around thirty minutes, accompanied by excitement and tension on his face – he might be able to win a slightly bigger handful of 2p's to go with the 2p already in his hand.

Eventually, the slot is chosen. The silence is broken. With a gesture as significant as the white smoke pouring from the Vatican, The Boy lowers his hand to touch the glass. Then he mutters the words I've been waiting for: 'It's gonna pay.'

And every time, without fail, it does. We were in the arcades for two hours and thirty-five minutes, at the same machine, the same slot. The Boy who, according to the

educational psychologist, had an attention span of approximately ninety seconds. And in that time he turned £0.16
into £3.44.

Kiss my arse, Dustin Hoffman, with your roulette tables and
card counting. Two-Pence-Pusher-Machine-Things are where
it's at.

MY SON'S NOT RAINMAN BLOG

I can't pretend that following the enlightened moment at the
school disco life suddenly became a breeze. It didn't, the same
old problems still reared their ugly heads, but I suppose they no
longer felt insurmountable; that was the difference.

School was still a huge difficulty in our lives and would
remain so for years to come. The same, familiar pattern started
again – OK at first, a few concerns and then a long, slow painful
spiral towards the inevitable.

Even though we were in a special school, the telephone calls
home were becoming more frequent. I had to leave the job in the
care home that had meant so much to me. Even on days when
I went to collect The Boy at normal home time, invariably he
was out of the classroom, either in the playground refusing to
come in or sitting with a member of the admin staff in one of
the offices. Things just weren't working out.

'We're a general special school. We feel that your son would
be better suited to a specialist autism provision.'

Sometimes the system can be bloody cruel.

The Boy was back home with me once more. After another few months of 'home tutoring' (oh, I'm sure the school inspectors would have been ever so impressed with Dad's curriculum) and me sending my traditional pain-in-the-arse emails chasing the local authority, another school was found in a neighbouring borough. (I've made it all sound so simple – it wasn't. Finding the right place involved eight months of endless bureaucracy, waiting for replies to emails that never came, having assessments, reading reports and so on. I can't bring myself to write about it because, frankly, it frustrates me beyond belief even thinking back to that time, knowing that every day an email was ignored or a deadline was missed was another day of my child's education that we would never, ever get back.)

The new school described itself as having specialist autism provision. Me and Mum were both incredibly nervous – this was now school number four and we weren't even out of primary. It had to work.

The Boy went for an assessment for a week to see how he settled. The assessment period was then extended to two weeks as they wanted to be absolutely certain they could meet his needs. I'd like to say that at the end of that period came a resounding 'Yes', but it was more of a 'We think so'. Beggars can't be choosers and all that… The cost to the local authority for this education? It was £43,000 a year. To give you some idea of just how expensive special-needs education is, at the time of writing in 2016 the exclusive Harrow school comes in at a mere snip of £37,350 – including boarding and laundry.

Things went fairly smoothly for the two-week assessment period. Then on the Monday, his official first day, The Boy calculated that the time had come for an attack. The element of surprise. Now was the time to bring out the big guns. This enemy had underestimated him. It was time for Shock-and-Awe.

By all accounts, it was apparently an impressive display. He pulled out everything in his arsenal. Kicking, punching, swearing, biting, spitting – he bombarded them with the lot. Wave after wave, barrage after barrage. Oh, yes, he'd show them who the superpower to be reckoned with was.

By the time I arrived to collect him at 3.30 p.m. the battle was over. I was called into the office for a full debriefing before heading off to assess the battleground and collect the wounded. As I opened the classroom door I was unsure what to expect. Tired and helpless, The Boy was flopped over a chair. The school uniform that had looked so new and fresh just hours earlier now hung from him like the battle fatigues of a veteran. He'd given everything. There was no more fight in him.

And standing next to him, the enemy. Mr Teacher.

'We made some wrong choices today, Dad,' Mr Teacher said, beaming away. 'But we've spoken about it and we're ready for a much better day tomorrow. I remember when I started at this school. And I was scared on my first day, too.'

And despite all my concerns and reservations, his smile told me that – for the time being – maybe we were in the right place. Far from being the enemy, maybe The Boy had met an ally. Someone who understood. Things might just be OK.

As we trundled out of the classroom with the remains of a smashed *Doctor Who* lunchbox in one hand and a bandaged home-school diary in the other, The Boy turned to me. 'I really like my new school, Daddy.'

Fingers crossed, son. Fingers crossed.

The official week one at the new school came to an end. It was an up-and-down week – a few triumphs scattered with 'some challenges'. Only one phone call home on Wednesday: result.

Then came Friday. My phone rang at about 1.00 p.m. It was Mr Teacher.

'I phone you when things are going wrong, so I thought I'd phone you when things are going right. He's having a brilliant day. No hitting, no biting, he's stayed in class all day, I'm really proud of him.'

Later that day when I went to collect The Boy there was still a part of me thinking how premature that call might have been. Old habits and all that… As I pulled up at the school The Boy came out of the gate. And there on his jumper was a sticker. 'Gold award'. And the romantic in me likes to think he was walking a little bit taller too. He got into the car and I read his home-school diary. At assembly this week he won the award for 'making good choices and controlling his actions.' I asked him if it made him feel happy. He started stammering, looking for the words that never seem to come when we talk about emotions of any kind. After an age, he blurted out, 'It made me feel like I was crying inside.' And we both just sat, silent, not sure who was more amazed that these words had tumbled out of him.

It was still early days, but Mr Teacher taught Dad a valuable lesson too that Friday. He taught him to believe in his son a bit more. And that night when The Boy went to bed I did what I'd seen other parents do in their houses. I stuck his gold award in pride of place on the fridge door.

And Dad cried a little bit too. On the inside, of course.

CHAPTER TWENTY-TWO

I Want to Tell You a Story

Last week at school was sports day. I hate sports day. In fact, there's one word too many in that sentence. I hate sports.

Maybe hate is too strong a word... I just don't see the point in it. Sports days are always around the same time as Wimbledon and that's another event that's largely escaped me. I try to care, really I do, but ultimately it's just a man or woman hitting a ball into a box painted on the floor with slightly more accuracy than some other man or woman hitting the ball into another box painted on the same floor. And then they sit down and drink some squash. I just don't get it.

I suppose it all comes down to whether or not you are a competitive person. I'm not. I couldn't support a football team because if my team won I'd feel sorry for the team that lost because I'd remember how that felt when it happened to me. I'd just want every result to be a draw and then everyone would be happy.

It's a bit like that age-old cliché that PE teachers have been rolling out for years – it isn't the winning that counts, it's the taking part. But when you were at school they never meant it. They couldn't hide the disappointment written all over their faces as you once more failed to stop the ball from crossing the goalmouth on a wet, cold, winter's day. It was never about the taking part.

So, sports day at The Boy's school.

The Boy took part in a few races. Even the running races. The Boy who I told you was now taking his wheelchair to school ran the 50 metres and the 100 metres. Don't forget now, consistently inconsistent… He came second in both races. And all right, it was out of three. And the boy who was third hadn't really grasped the concept of the race – but none of that mattered in the slightest.

Then came the long jump. Or to give it its full title, Walking Through A Sandpit. There might not have been much jumping, but that's what made the day so special – none of it mattered, each competitor was cheered on like an Olympian by parents and teachers alike.

Then the javelin. Or Chucking a Foam Dart in a Field. The Boy excelled at this. He was offered three attempts, but he decided one was enough. You can have too much of a good thing.

Then, the final event. The high jump. Or Throwing Yourself Onto a Mattress. Like so many of the other competitors, The

Boy's style was slightly less than conventional. But you couldn't doubt his commitment as he flung himself onto that mattress like a stunt man in a Hollywood blockbuster.

It was a brilliant day, marred only by one thing. Parents' race. I can't tell you who won, as I was hiding behind a gazebo at the time. It's true what they say, it's the taking part that matters…

A nd so I suppose I'd finally made my peace with The Boy's diagnosis, some years after it happened. Even now it bothers me sometimes, often creeping up unawares when I watch him struggle with some aspect of his life, but for the most part now there is acceptance. Largely because I recognize that I can never expect him to accept it and lead a happy adult life if those around him don't. We've tried talking about what it means to be autistic, about having a brain that is just wired differently, but for now the understanding isn't there. We go to a special school because we have a problem with our legs and that's OK. The rest will come when the time is ready.

Gradually, I'd finally begun to recognize the importance of doing things for me, too. As carers we invariably put our own needs to one side, seemingly flagellating ourselves for the greater good. With hindsight I'd become quite lonely, isolated even – my entire life was spent sat waiting for the school to ring or to take my shift on watch duty in the playground. I began to realize that the best way to do something for us was to do something for me.

Many years ago, just before I became ill, I dabbled in stand-up comedy. I did it for a few months and it turned out I was quite good at it. I'd only done a handful of gigs and I found myself in the final of a national competition to find the best new comedian in the UK. On the night itself I died on my arse. Horrifically. And then I became ill, and then autism and all the rest of it got in the way. The stand-up just petered out.

There was something about stand-up comedy, though, that got under my skin. I'm not sure what it was, whether it was the risk involved or the buzz – when it goes well there's nothing better, but when it goes bad… it goes bad. I guess that's the thrill of it – over time I may well get better at it, but the prospect of dying onstage is never far away.

I quietly returned to stand-up over the course of a few months. Small gigs in London, ten minutes here, fifteen minutes there, while The Boy was at his mum's house. I enjoyed it.

I had heard comedians talk of 'finding their voice' onstage – tapping into that unique viewpoint of the world that often makes the best comedians who they are. I'm not entirely sure I've ever really tapped into mine, but I know I felt far more comfortable onstage than I had done years before. Maybe I was older or wiser or maybe I cared a little bit less about what people thought of me and that freed me up a bit. Or maybe I just enjoyed being out of the house sometimes.

For me, the best comedians have always had a truth to their material. Often there will be exaggeration or embellishment and the character onstage isn't quite the same person offstage, no matter how convincing they might appear, but their viewpoint is rooted in a truth about how they see the world. I talked about The Boy in my stand-up. Most of it was largely about our life together – the foibles of family life. The disability, I left that out, but I always felt like I wasn't being true to The Boy for not including it, like I was editing our lives to make them more palatable to people.

And then came that fateful gig in central London, the one in which I mentioned his autism, as I told you at the beginning of the book. I'd like to take you back to that moment again because I really didn't know at the time the impact that night would have on our lives.

I can't remember too much about the gig itself. I remember the compere doing a great job, the comic before me ripping up the room and me backstage thinking they sounded like a lovely, up-for-it crowd. I was going to do my usual stuff, except this time I wasn't going to hide his autism.

What I remember best is the utter absence of laughter from the one hundred and thirty faces staring back at me. I said before that there was silence in the room. That's not true, of course. I could hear the sound of the barman at the far side squirting Diet Pepsi into a glass, the faint hum of the hand dryer from the far-off toilet filling the room where the laughter should have been. And then the quandary. I was four minutes in and booked for a twenty-minute set. Should I front this out or limp off to the side admitting defeat and facing the wrath of the promoter? I made it to eight painful minutes, I'd won back a table at the front, but the rest of the room either sat in awkwardness or talked among themselves. To this day I'm not sure which is worse as a comic – an attentive but silent audience or the hum of conversation while I'm just ignored completely.

I headed backstage – not really making eye-contact with the other comics – just in time to hear the compere getting laughs from the room once more.

After an awkward handshake with the promoter, I went to leave, the voice in my head telling me over and over that it was OK and that I'd never see any of those people again. And then I discovered the only way out of the venue was back through the room I'd just died in. I swallowed my pride and went for it.

I made it through the room relatively unscathed, save for the odd look, and saw freedom in the shape of the exit ahead of me. As I got there, a man walked back in from the toilets. He held the door open for me. 'That shit you spoke about up there, was that stuff true?' he said to me as I headed out.

I nodded back, almost apologetically.

'F*cking hell,' he said, almost laughing to himself, shaking his head.

You know the rest: I headed home, trying to convince myself that it didn't matter, their reaction was nothing personal about The Boy. I'd pick myself up and carry on. Everything was OK.

A week later, having cancelled almost all the gigs in the diary, there was just one more I had to do, because it was too late to pull out. I was compering; it was a lovely room with a lovely bunch of comics and it felt like the perfect antidote to the car crash a week earlier. I sat and chatted with the other acts in the green room, telling them about what had happened the week before.

'You should write an Edinburgh show about you and your son,' one comic said. 'Take it to the Fringe. There isn't the pressure of a club night as you have fifty minutes, you have more time to tell your story and it should be told. Do it.'

Then the headline comic that night said, 'Come on, do it. You could call it "My Son's Not Rainman".' Somewhere, a light went on.

The next day I registered the domain name. I asked an old friend if she'd direct the show. She said 'Yes'. It was now April and I was looking at heading to Edinburgh in August the following year. My friend booked a slot at a theatre in London for October previews, six months away. All I had to do was write the show.

At the same time I had a domain name just sitting there doing nothing. I thought I'd start up a blog about us, tell people about the highlights and lowlights. But mainly it was to share some of the brilliantly funny aspects of our lives. I wasn't completely selfless in all this – my reasons were as much about the two of us as they were about the 'greater good'. If there was one thing the years in therapy taught me (no matter how much the cynic in me tried to fight it), it was that focusing on the positive can only be a good thing. This was as much about us as it was everyone else.

After two months of blogging I had a handful of followers. Three of them were my brothers. Then slowly, slowly, things started to pick up. I found I enjoyed writing, something I'd not done since leaving school. After four months, I was elated when my visitor count reached double figures.

October crept up quicker than I'd hoped, as did the date of the first preview of the show. At that point it was far from ready. I'd discovered that writing a comedy around the subject was trickier than I first thought, especially as I was on the outside looking in. I suppose that was the problem – I never really wanted it to be 'about autism' or 'about disability' – I just wanted it to be 'about us', of which the rest was only a part. The fear that I would be seen to be mocking people terrified me. Ours was very much a story about acceptance.

The first previews came and went. They weren't entirely successful. 'Needs more jokes,' my friends said helpfully. And despite my best efforts, some parts of the show felt cruel, exactly what I'd been trying to avoid; other bits were schmaltzy where I'd over-egged the 'I love my son and this comes from a good place' angle.

Just after the Christmas period, I received a message from a journalist who worked for the disability section of the BBC website. She'd been reading the blog for a while, and had tried to come to the preview show earlier. 'Will you write us a guest blog? We're looking for something around parenting a child with disabilities in half-term.'

I was flattered and, of course, I said I would. I wrote about me and The Boy going ten-pin bowling. On the Friday when it was due to go online, I received a message from the journalist. 'Hi John, your article has been selected for the main BBC News website. I'm not sure when publication will be.' I wasn't entirely sure from the tone of the message if this was a good thing or not, so I just had to wait and see.

The next day I woke with my phone going crazy. I'm not sure why the article became as successful as it did. Maybe it was because someone had decided to use the attention-grabbing headline 'Fortnight of fear' (not a decision I'd have made), but there it was, online. It became the second most-read article on the BBC website that day, with just under one million impressions. In one day alone my own blog suddenly had 340,000 hits.

Then the emails started arriving – other parents reading the blog and recognizing their own child, people with no link to autism at all who wanted to know more, autistics themselves sharing their own stories. So many emails telling me what an amazing, incredible son I had, and how incredibly proud I should be.

I'm not going to go on and on about the show and blog for fear of being an unbearable bore, but the impact of people recognizing just what a wonderful, brilliant being The Boy is, can never be underestimated. When you've spent your life with people constantly finding the negative and never looking past it to see just what's inside, the sudden outpouring by people who recognized his talents, his humour, his heart and his very soul… let's just say it was, and has continued to be, incredibly special.

The show went well at the Edinburgh Fringe. Since then I've performed it up and down the land, in comedy clubs and at other events – the National Autistic Society's conference, head teachers' conferences, and so on. An excerpt of the show recorded for Radio 4 was selected by the BBC as one of their 'magic moments of radio 2015'. The Boy who took so long to find his voice was finally being heard.

And I suppose this book is the culmination of it all. It's funny, I was completing a form the other day for school and I needed to add my occupation. I had to think about it. What am I now? Am I a comedian? A writer? Instead I opted for that horrible term, 'carer'. But really, I'm not that either. I'm just Dad. And there's no better job in the world.

CHAPTER TWENTY-THREE

Tomorrow

Our weekend away in a caravan was a great break for both of us. Sometimes it takes going away for you to recognize the changes that go unnoticed day to day. Like when I visit my mum who I haven't seen for four months and she points straight away to that seven pound weight gain I thought I'd been quietly getting away with.

And so it was with revisiting a caravan park we hadn't been to for a while. I'd forgotten the previous battles in getting out of the swimming pool, the altercations in the play area and the screams echoing around the bowling alley. For the most part, this time they were absent.

Although the change in behaviour was delightful to see, I'm still unsure if the cause is a good thing. It was always social interactions with other children that created the problems – on the dance floor in the evening, across a ball pit – that's where the difficulties came. When this little boy, so desperate to make friends and interact, didn't have the first clue how to do any of it. While other parents sat chatting and drinking he was the child I never dared take my eye off. Hearing a scream from the ball pit and seeing a distressed toddler fleeing the scene clutching their wound and then discovering the culprit alone inside, confused, scared and mystified, having got it all wrong again.

But this time there were no social interactions to worry about. And that's the bit I'm not sure is good. Yes, it made for a less stressful time, but was the lack of attempting social interaction just his age or because he's learnt that there's no point trying to get along with people because it's all just too hard and confusing?

Either way, the two of us still had a great time, revisiting old haunts. We sat in the same seats we always sat in when we went for dinner. The Boy told me which machines were new and which had been moved in the arcades, and he pointed out the caravan we stayed in three years ago even though it wasn't in its original spot and there were three hundred other caravans in that park which looked exactly the same to me.

He had jobs to do this holiday too. Chores. He likes the responsibility, the sense of being in charge. 'I'm getting a big boy now,' became one of his favourite phrases as he turned the lights off or locked the caravan each time we went out (granted, the time we went out all day it might have been more secure if the door had actually been closed, but we'll let it go).

And he'd never seemed older than when we went for dinner on the Friday evening. Clutching his pack of playing cards he even sat alone while I went to the bar to order. Two adult meals. The kids' menu was always going to be out of bounds since my own flashbacks of sitting in a Little Chef while my dad tried to convince a waitress that the fifteen-year-old and two thirteen-year-olds sitting in front of her were nine years of age. Maybe if my elder brother had shaved that morning we might have got away with it.

After dinner and his favourite card game (for the record, I won), The Boy was ready to head back to the caravan. No bingo, no playing with other children this time. And, as we went to leave, from out of nowhere came the highlight of the holiday. 'Now I'm a big boy,' he said as he watched me putting the cards back in their case, 'can I have my own packet of mints?'

Oh, son, just writing that line makes me smile more than anything. I always carry a packet of mints with me. I'm not even sure why, it's just something my dad always did, especially in the latter years when he took to stopping smoking once a fortnight. Other families pass on heirlooms and relics across the generations. Ours pass on mints. And, as we walked into the shop to buy the confectionery of choice, it felt like his coming of age ceremony, his very own bar mitzvah.

And if you were there that night, you might well have witnessed the momentous occasion. At 7.23 p.m. on Friday, 28 March, in a caravan park in south-east England, a young man walked out of the corner shop and silently slipped a packet of Trebor Extra Strong Mints into his pocket. Turning towards the setting sun, he headed for home with the caravan key in his hand and the whole world at his feet.

MY SON'S NOT RAINMAN BLOG

I t's the night before The Boy's thirteenth birthday. And this is where our story ends. In a few hours' time, The Boy becomes The Teen and it's such a cliché but I can't believe how the time has gone. People always say that about their children – one minute they're born, then they're leaving home and their childhood has gone in the blink of an eye. But if I'm honest, for years that wasn't the case. Time stood still for far too long and there were days in it all that I thought would never end. It's fair to say we've both been on a journey these past years.

He's taller than his mum now. I buy the same size socks for both of us. He borrowed a T-shirt of mine the other day. Mind you, we still watch far too much *Power Rangers*; that one will be a work in progress for some time to come. For so long, I could never picture him as an adult. I couldn't contemplate this child, this young boy, as a grown man. But I can see it now. And rather than fill me with fear and dread as it used to, it excites me. I have glimpses of the kind of adult he might become. The anger still needs work, there's no doubt. And the anxiety too, I wish that would bugger off at some point. But the kindness, the gentleness, the sense of humour...

Oh son, what a fine man you are growing up to be.

I still think of my own dad nowadays too. Maybe I understand him more, now I've been a parent myself for a few years. And I suppose my view of him is a bit more honest than it used to be. He will forever be on a pedestal because he was My Dad and because I had a love for him that makes my heart sing and drowns my eyes with tears whenever I think of his big, brilliant face. He wasn't perfect, though. And I'm slowly realizing that not being perfect, that's OK too. I see him in The Boy more and more. The way The Boy throws his head back and laughs. The way he does that funny thing with his lips when he's concentrating. Dad's never far away.

And so it's time to hand things over to The Boy. The story ends here, because it isn't my story to tell anymore. It's his. When I first came up with the idea of this book, I was unsure of the journey it would take us on. Yet the one bit I was clear about was the ending; that was never going to change. This is how I described the last chapter:

'The Boy. The final word will go to him. I don't know what this chapter will be. It could be a sentence, a paragraph, a page. It might even just be a drawing. But it will be his.'

And so, it's over to you son. Be brilliant. Dad x

CHAPTER TWENTY-FOUR

My Page

I cant Draw
power rangers

The end
(of the beginning)

AUTHOR'S NOTE

The use of language can often be a contentious issue, particularly when you are attempting to describe a condition that affects so many people in so many different ways. It's 2016 as I write this but, should you be picking this book up twenty years from now, I am sure there is terminology used that makes you shudder; phrases that have long been consigned to history. Even in the few years I have been writing on the subject of autism, there is much that has changed – just one example, is The Boy someone 'with autism' or is he 'autistic'? I've largely chosen the latter, as I feel that is what he is most comfortable with. And that has been my benchmark throughout the book – I have attempted to use language that I feel he best identifies with, but I recognize that may not be the same for everyone.

ACKNOWLEDGEMENTS

None of this would have been possible without the support of a huge number of people to whom I owe a very heartfelt thank you.

To the wonderful comedian Mary Bourke, the headliner who nonchalantly said to me that night in the green room, 'You should call it "My Son's Not Rainman". The rest, as they say...

To Anna Crilly, my lovely friend who started it all by booking the theatre, agreeing to direct the show and making sure I actually turned up on the night.

To Vicki Salter from my literary agent, Barbara Levy, who contacted me after seeing me perform one night in a working men's club on the south coast of England. She asked if I'd considered turning the blog into a book. Until that point, I hadn't.

The kindness, support and wisdom from her and Barbara have been invaluable.

To my ever patient publisher, Hugh Barker at Michael O'Mara Books, who I instantly warmed to because he took me out for a cup of coffee at our initial meeting as he'd finally got his first-ever company credit card and wanted to test it out.

To Fiona Slater, my editor. Together with Hugh, she has often taken on the role of therapist. Her guidance, understanding and genuine consideration for what is best for The Boy is the only reason this book exists at all.

To my dear family and friends, who have fielded endless panicking phone calls over many months, if not years. In particular to Nena, Dave, Greg, Kuljit, Saskia, Anna, Bethany, Annette and Tracey. My world would be a far duller place without each of you in it and I promise I will never mention the bloody book again.

And finally to Connor, Joe, Ted, George, Molly, Olly, Asha and Jacob. I can't even begin to tell each of you how much joy you have brought into our world. Thank you for being the finest cousins and friends any little boy could hope for.

ABOUT CONNOR SPARROWHAWK AND JUSTICE FOR LB

T his book is dedicated to the memory of Connor Sparrowhawk. Connor was a fit and healthy young man who loved buses, London, the Eddie Stobart haulage company and speaking his mind. He lived in Oxford, England, and was in the sixth form of a local special school. He was diagnosed with autism, learning disabilities and epilepsy.

Connor's mum, Sara, created a blog online in which he was affectionately known as Laughing Boy (LB). It was through this blog and her wonderful writing that I, and countless others, felt as if we got to know LB in some small way. LB's mood changed as he approached adulthood and on 19 March 2013 he was admitted to hospital, the STATT (Short Term Assessment and Treatment Team) inpatient unit run by Southern Health NHS Foundation Trust.

LB drowned in the bath in the inpatient unit on 4 July 2013. An entirely preventable death. Since Connor's death, his family and a small team of incredibly dedicated supporters have campaigned endlessly under the Justice for LB banner, not only to ensure a full investigation took place into his death, but to further improve the life opportunities of all people with learning disabilities.

In October 2015 the jury at Connor's inquest concluded that neglect and very serious failings contributed to his death. Finally, in June 2016, Southern Health NHS Foundation Trust accepted responsibility for the death of Connor Sparrowhawk.

The Justice for LB campaign continues to push for further assurances that what happened to Connor will not happen to others. They also want to see proper informed debate about the status of learning disabled adults as full citizens in the UK, involving and led by learning disabled people and their families.

justiceforlb.org
www.facebook.com/justiceforLB
www.twitter.com/justiceforLB

ABOUT EXPRESS CIC

In 2013 I was delighted to become patron of Express CIC. They are a small, not-for-profit organization based in southwest London. Their goal is to provide a café/hub where young people with autism and their families/carers can feel welcome and secure in their local community. A place for everyone.

Their vision is to offer employment opportunities for both autistic people and their carers and to become a thriving centre at the heart of the community. A place where sensory needs are taken into account, combined with quiet zones and play areas. It's very early days for them and, although I am increasingly frustrated and bamboozled on their behalf by the endless bureaucracy that seems to stand in the way of brilliant community projects, I'm genuinely thrilled to be involved and I have no doubt that with the passion and drive of those behind it,

Express will thrive and prosper as it should. In the three years since forming, they have already firmly established themselves as a lifeline to many families, running art therapy classes, parent support groups, a newly formed dad's group and groups for siblings too.

Five per cent of all author profits from this book will go to Express CIC.

expresscic.org.uk
www.facebook.com/expresscic
www.twitter.com/expresscic

ABOUT THE AUTHOR

John Williams has had far too many jobs to list, ranging from working on the factory floor of a chicken processing plant to being a graphic designer for a City firm. He has worked as a comedian on and off for around twelve years, fitting it in around childcare. As a public speaker he has appeared at national conferences and events throughout the UK and Europe, and featured extensively on BBC Radio 4. *My Son's Not Rainman* is his first book, and you can find his blog at www.mysonsnotrainman.com. He is appalling at writing about himself in the third person, but is brilliant at dance-offs.